DON'T GET TOO COMFORTABLE

Also by David Rakoff

Fraud

David
Rakoff

DON'T GET TOO COMFORTABLE

DOUBLEDAY

New York London Toronto Sydney Auckland

PUBLISHED BY DOUBLEDAY

a division of Random House, Inc.

1745 Broadway, New York, New York 10019

DOUBLEDAY and the portrayal of an anchor with a dolphin are trademarks
of Doubleday, a division of Random House, Inc.

Some of the pieces herein began their lives elsewhere in different forms:
"Sesión Privada" in *Details*; "Wildman" in *Seed*; "As It Is in Heaven,"
"Beat Me, Daddy," "Whatsizface," and "Off We're Gonna Shuffle" in *GQ*;
"J.D.V., M.I.A.," "Martha, My Dear," and "Faster" on *This American Life*;
and "I Can't Get It for You Wholesale" in *Harper's Bazaar*.

ISBN: 0-7394-6698-4

ISBN: 978-0-7394-6698-8

FOR IRENE SKOLNICK

Contents

CONTENTS

"I lived in the Palace of Sans-Souci, where sorrow is not allowed to enter. In the daytime I played with my companions in the garden, and in the evening I led the dance in the Great Hall. Round the garden ran a very lofty wall, but I never cared to ask what lay beyond it, everything about me was so beautiful. My courtiers called me the Happy Prince, and happy indeed I was, if pleasure be happiness."

—Oscar Wilde, "The Happy Prince"

London, May 9—Give an infinite number of monkeys an infinite number of typewriters, the theory goes, and they will produce the complete works of Shakespeare. Give six monkeys one computer for a month, and they will make a mess. Researchers at Plymouth University in England reported this week that monkeys left alone with a computer failed to produce a single word. "They pressed a lot of S's," said Mike Phillips, a researcher in the project which was paid for by the Arts Council. The researchers left a computer in the monkey enclosure at Paignton Zoo in southwest England, home to six Sulawesi crested macaques. Then they waited. Eventually, the monkeys produced only five pages of text, primarily filled with the letter S. At the end, a few A's, J's, L's and M's were struck. "Another thing they were interested in was defecating and urinating all over the keyboard," Mr. Phillips added.

—Associated Press

DON'T GET TOO COMFORTABLE

LOVE IT OR LEAVE IT

George W. Bush made me want to be an American. It was a need I had not known before. A desire that came over me in a rush one day, not unlike that of the pencil-necked honors student suddenly overwhelmed with the inexplicable urge to make a daily gift of his lunch money to the schoolyard tough. I have lived in the United States, first as a student then as a resident alien, under numerous other administrations, including what I once thought of as the nadir of all time: the Cajun-scented, plague-ravaged Reagan eighties in New York; horrible, black years of red fish and blue drinks. A time when greed was magically transformed from vice to virtue. And after that the even greedier nineties, when the money flowed like water and everybody's boat rose with the tide (except, of course, for those forgotten souls who had been provided not with boats but with stones, and no one told them. Oh well, *tra la*), and all through that time, aside from having to make sure not to get myself arrested at demonstrations, I was sufficiently satisfied with a civic life of paying taxes and the occasional protest.

But George changed all that. Even though I am not a Muslim and I come from a country that enjoys cordial relations with the United States, I no longer felt safe being here as just a lawful permanent resident. Under the cudgel-like Patriot Act, a shoot-first-ask-questions-later bit of legislation, there are residents who have been here since childhood, other folks who sired American-born children, who have found themselves deported—often to countries of which they have almost no firsthand knowledge—for the most minor, not remotely terrorist-related infractions. Those people are never coming back, at least not during this administration. I don't want to be put out of my home, and like it or not this is my home. I have been here longer than I haven't. After twenty-two years, it seemed a little bit coy to still be playing the Canadian card. I felt like the butt of that old joke about the proper lady who, when asked if she would have sex with a strange man for a million dollars, allows that yes she would do it. But when asked if she would do the same thing for a can of Schlitz and a plastic sleeve of beer nuts, reels back with an affronted, "What do you think I am?" to which the response is, "Madam, we have already established what you are. Now we're just quibbling about the price." Becoming a citizen merely names a state of affairs already in place for a long time.

Even so, once I reach my decision, I don't make my intentions widely known. I tell almost no one, especially no one in Canada. You can only know this if you grew up in a country directly adjacent to a globally dominating, culturally obliterating economic behemoth, but becoming an American feels like some kind of defeat. Another one bites the dust.

THE NATURALIZATION APPLICATION can be downloaded directly from the government's website. It is ten pages long but can be filled out over the course of an industrious day or two. It takes me four months and one week. I got delayed twice, although not by the usual pitfalls of questions requiring a lot of documentation from over a long period. I have no problem, for example, with Part 7, Section C, in which I have to account for every trip I have taken out of the United States of more than twenty-four-hours' duration for the last ten years, including every weekend jaunt to Canada to see the family. I have kept every datebook I have ever owned. I pore over a decade's worth of pages and list all of my travels from most recent backward. I create a table with columns, listing exact dates of departure and return, plus my destination. It is a document of such surpassing beauty, it is virtually scented. Not since I threaded puffy orange yarn through the punched holes of my fourth-grade book reports have I so shamelessly tried to placate authority with meaningless externals.

No, my first hang-up occurs at Part 10, Section G, question

33: *Are you a male who lived in the United States at any time between your 18th and 26th birthdays in any status except as a lawful nonimmigrant?* I make my living with words and yet I cannot for the life of me begin to parse this question with its imbedded double negatives and hypotheticals. How are any nonnative speakers managing to become citizens, I wonder? Part of my clouded judgment is due to fear. I don't want to piss them off, and I am worried that a wrong answer will immediately feed my name into some database for a wiretap, a tax audit, or an automatic years-long "misplacement" of my application; some casual gratuitous harassment that a thuggish administration might decide to visit upon someone they identified as a troublemaker. I spend an entire afternoon trying to map the grammar and come away with nothing but a headache and no idea. This is in early March. I put the form away in my drawer and forget about it, my dreams of inalienable rights felled by just one question. I put all thoughts of citizenship out of my head, until one evening in July, four months later, when, as I'm dropping off to sleep, the clauses fall into place and the lock turns and I realize the answer is a simple "no." With inordinate self-satisfaction, I soldier on. Have I ever been a habitual drunkard? I have not. A prostitute, a procurer, or a bigamist? Nuh-uh. Did I in any way aid, abet, support, work for, or claim membership in the Nazi government of Germany between March 23, 1933, and May 8, 1945? *Nein!* Do I understand and support the Constitution? You betcha. If the law required it, would I be willing to bear arms on behalf of the United States?

Again I stop. The same headache as before marches its little foot soldiers across my cranium. I put the application back into the drawer and return to my bed, not picking it up again until seven days later when I surprise myself by checking "yes."

I figure it's grass soup. Grass soup is exactly what it sounds like. It's a recipe for food of last resort that my father apparently has squirreled away somewhere. I have never actually seen this recipe, but it was referred to fairly often when I was a child. Should everything else turn to shit, we could always derive sustenance from nutritious grass soup! At heart, it's an anxious, romantic fantasy that disaster and total financial ruin lurk just around the corner, but when they do come, they will have all the stark beauty and domestic fine feeling of a Dickens novel. Young Tiny Tim's palsied hand lifting a spoon to his rosebud mouth. "What delicious grass soup. I must be getting better after all," he will say, putting on a good show of it just as he expires, the tin utensil clattering to the rough wood table.

A grass-soup situation is a self-dramatizing one based on such a poorly imagined and improbable premise as to render it beneath consideration. Michael Jackson saying with no apparent irony, for example, that were he to wake up one day to find all the children in the world gone, he would throw himself out the window. Mr. Jackson's statement doesn't really take into consideration that a planet devoid of tots would likely be just one link in a chain of geopolitical events so cataclysmic, that to assume the presence of an intact building with an intact window out of which to throw himself is plain idiotic. As for grass soup itself, from what I've seen on the news, by the time you're reduced to using the lawn for food, any grass that isn't already gone—either parched to death or napalmed into oblivion—is probably best eaten on the run.

All by way of saying, that if there ever came a time when the government of my new homeland was actually calling up the forty-something asking-and-telling homosexuals with hypo-active thyroids to take up arms, something very calamitous indeed will have to have happened. The streets would likely be running with blood, and such moral gray areas as might have existed at other times will seem either so beside the point that I will join the fight, or so terrifying and appallingly beyond the pale that I'd either already be dead or underground.

For most of my life, I would have automatically said that I would opt for conscientious objector status, and in general, I still would. But the spirit of the question is would I *ever*, and there are instances where I might. If immediate intervention would have circumvented the genocide in Rwanda or stopped the Janjaweed in Darfur, would I choose pacifism? Of course not. Scott Simon, the reporter for National Public Radio and a committed lifelong Quaker, has written that it took looking into mass graves in former Yugoslavia to convince him that force is sometimes the only option to deter our species' murderous impulses.

While we're on the subject of the horrors of war, and humanity's most poisonous and least charitable attributes, let us not forget to mention Barbara Bush (that would be former First Lady and presidential mother as opposed to W's liquor-swilling, Girl Gone Wild, human ashtray of a daughter. I'm sorry, that's not fair. I've no idea if she smokes). When the administration censored images of the flag-draped coffins of the young men and women being killed in Iraq—purportedly to respect "the privacy of the families" and not to minimize and cover up the true nature and consequences of the war—the family matriarch expressed her support for what was ultimately her son's decision by saying on *Good Morning America* on March 18, 2003, "Why should we hear about body bags and deaths? I mean, it's not relevant. So why should I waste my beautiful mind on something like that?"

Mrs. Bush is not getting any younger. When she eventually ceases to walk among us we will undoubtedly see photographs of *her* flag-draped coffin. Whatever obituaries that run will admiringly mention those wizened, dynastic loins of hers and praise her staunch refusal to color her hair or glamorize her image. But will they remember this particular statement of hers, this "Let them eat cake" for the twenty-first century? Unlikely, since it received far too little play and definitely insufficient outrage when she said it. So let us promise herewith to never forget her callous disregard for other parents' children while her own son was sending them to make the ultimate sacrifice, while asking of the rest of us little more than to promise to go shopping. Commit the quote to memory and say it whenever her name comes up. Remind others how she lacked even the bare minimum of human integrity, the most

basic requirement of decency that says if you support a war,
you should be willing, if not to join those nineteen-year-olds
yourself, then at least, *at the very least,* to acknowledge that
said war was actually going on. Stupid fucking cow.

So that's why I answered "yes." But, like I said, it is grass
soup. (I hope.)

THERE HAS BEEN much talk about a post–September 11
backlog of applications and how I should expect to wait far
longer than the usual year. But ten months after filing, I am
notified that I have been provisionally approved, pending an
interview. I am to report to the Bureau of Citizenship and
Immigration Services at Federal Plaza. It is a scorcher of a
May day when I go downtown. Even now there are equivalents of first class and steerage. Those of us with scheduled
appointments are immediately ushered inside and through the
metal detectors, while the line of people who have just shown
up snakes around the block. I check in at the window and am
asked if, before starting the official process of my glorious,
butterfly-like transformation into David Rakoff, American, I'd
like to change my name. The hairy-knuckled, pinkie-ringed
lawyer for a Vietnamese fellow behind me nudges his client
and says, "Hear that? You wanna change your name? To
George Bush? Saddam Hussein? Anything you want. Haw
haw," he laughs, clapping his client on the back. The young
man shoots me an apologetic look to suggest that, yes, even
with the obvious cultural and language barriers, he knows that
he has unwittingly hired a shithead.

There are about fifty of us waiting for our interviews. Many people are in their best clothes. I wonder if I've adversely affected my chances by having opted for comfort in Levi's and sneakers, but so long as the Russian woman in her early forties is across from me, I have nothing to worry about. She wears painted-on acid-wash jeans, white stilettos, and a tight blouse of sheer leopard-print fabric. The sleeves are designed as a series of irregular tatters clinging to her arms, as if she's just come from tearing the hide off of the back of an actual leopard. A really slutty leopard.

My name is called, and Agent Morales brings me back into her office. From her window I can see the Brooklyn Bridge, hazy under a humid sky the color of a soiled shirt collar. Agent Morales's desk is crowded with small plaster figures of cherubic children holding fishing poles, polka-dot-hankie hobo bundles, small wicker picnic baskets, etc. The walls, however, are almost completely bare. Perhaps it's bureau policy, but all of those typical examples of office humor—that in other work environments might get their own piece of paper, perhaps with Garfield or Dilbert saying them—have all been printed onto the same 8½ × 11 sheet and listed like bullets in a PowerPoint presentation. There are old standbys like "You don't have to be crazy to work here, but it sure helps," along with some gags that are new to me: "Chocolate, coffee, men: some things are just better rich" and "I'm out of estrogen and I have a gun!"—the latter which frankly seems to push the envelope for acceptable discourse in a government office.

She has me raise my right hand while swearing to tell the

truth. That's it, no Bible, no Koran, no sacred text of any sort to solidify my oath. Perhaps the increased blood flow from my upheld arm down into my heart is enough to safeguard against perjury. She questions me about any potential criminal past. (A boy could get ideas, or at least a distorted view of his own allure, seeing as how regularly I am asked if I have ever turned tricks.) Agent Morales then administers my citizenship test. Along with my application, I downloaded the list of one hundred possible questions, any handful of which they might choose to ask. Some of them are incredibly basic, like when is Independence Day, while others delve more deeply into the three branches of government, or ask you to name some of the better-known amendments.

Here are the four questions I am asked: What do the stripes on the flag represent? What were the original states called? What is the judiciary? And, who takes over if the president dies?

"Dick Cheney, God help us," I answer with a shudder. Agent Morales gives me a small half smile. She then has me write down on a piece of paper, "I watch the news every day." It's the literacy test, the final hurdle of the interview. She looks at it and, picking up my application, she compares them, her eyes going back and forth between the two documents.

"Wait a second. Who wrote your application?" she asks, confused.

"I did, but I was really, really careful."

"Oh my God," she says, almost with relief. " 'Cause the writing is so different. We couldn't believe it, your application was so tidy. It looked so good, and *this* was so good . . ." she says, unfolding my painstaking table of trips outside the country. She reads through it once more, as if reminiscing over a pleasant memory. Pathetically, in that moment, being approved for citizenship is secondary to the thrill that her kind words about my penmanship give me. I am out of there within five minutes, a provisional American. I have now only to wait for my swearing in. Exiting the same door onto lower Broadway that I did almost exactly ten years previously when I got my green card, the same bleakness overtakes me. It is a feeling more unrooted than mere statelessness. It's as though all my moorings have been cut. Any connection that I might have had to anything or anyone has been, for the moment, severed. It's a cold realization that I am now, as indeed I always have been, an official unit of one.

COINCIDENTALLY, CANADIAN-BORN newscaster Peter Jennings also became a citizen around the same time, after almost forty years in the United States. According to the papers, his swearing in took place in a swanky Manhattan courthouse. I, on the other hand, am forced to catch the 6:55 a.m. train to Hempstead, Long Island. My friend Sarah, a self-described civics nerd, very sweetly agrees to come with me. She is a good deal more excited than I am. This all feels like monumentally bad timing, or possibly the entirely wrong move altogether. Just two days prior, the front page of the paper had two news stories. The first was about how Canada was on the brink of legalizing gay marriage, and the second told of an appeals

court in the District of Columbia Circuit that ruled that the
detainees at Guantánamo Bay are legally outside the reach of
the protections of the Constitution.

The INS center, a one-story sprawl devoid of character, fits
into its very unprepossessing surroundings of a highway of
strip malls with empty storefronts. Still, the air is electric with
a sense of occasion as we line up at the door. No one has come
alone and people are dressed to the nines. We are separated
from our friends and family and pass through the final sheep
dip before becoming Americans. I have to answer once again
whether, in the intervening four weeks between my interview
and now, I have become a dipsomaniac, a whore, or traveled
backward in time to willingly participate in Kristallnacht. They
take back my green card, which after ten years is barely holding up. It was always government property. There is a strange
lightness I feel having turned in the small laminated object
that has been on my person for an entire decade. Something
has been lanced. For the brief walk from this anteroom to the
main auditorium, I am a completely undocumented human.
The only picture ID I have is my gym membership and it has
my name spelled wrong.

There is absolutely nothing on the walls of the huge
fluorescent-lit, dropped-ceiling room into which we are corralled. It's the new federalist architecture. Even travel agen-
cies give out free posters of the Grand Canyon or the Chicago
loop at night. Alternately, how hard could it be to get a bunch
of schoolchildren in to paint a lousy mural of some politically
neutral rainbows and trees? Our guests are already seated way

in the back; I cannot find Sarah in the sea of faces. I am grateful for the newspaper I have brought with me as it takes well over an hour for everyone to register and find their seats. Across the aisle from me, one of my fellow soon-to-be new citizens has a paperback. He is reading *American Psycho*. Give me your tired, your poor, your huddled masses yearning to read about a murderous yuppie dispatching live rodents into women's vaginas. Welcome, friend.

I catnap a little and one of the guards turns on a boom box perched on a chair for the musical prelude. A typical pompy instrumental of "The Star-Spangled Banner," followed by a very atypical "America the Beautiful" rendered in a minor-key full-strings orchestration straight out of a forties noir. Three women and one man then get up on the dais. The man checks that everyone has turned in all their documents. It's a minor federal offense to keep them. "Your old passports from the countries you came from are souvenirs and can never be used again." The people in the back are instructed to applaud loudly, people with cameras are told to take lots of pictures. There is pretty well only joy in this room, save for some extreme Canadian ambivalence.

They lead us in the Pledge of Allegiance. I leave off "under God" as I say it. Oh, maverick! I feel about as renegade as the mohawked young "anarchist" I once watched walking up Third Avenue on a Saturday evening. For some reason the streets were choked with limousines that night. My young friend spat contemptuously at each one that sat unoccupied and parked, while letting the peopled vehicles go saliva free.

To lead us in singing the national anthem for our first time as Americans, we have a choir. Not a real choir, but a group of employees who come up to the front. We sing and I cry, although I'm not sure why. I'm clearly overcome by something. It's a combination of guilt over having shown insufficient appreciation for my origins, of feeling very much alone in the world, and—I am not proud to say—of constructing life-and-death grass-soup scenarios for the immigrants standing around me. Strangely, no one else that I can see sheds a tear. Perhaps it is because they are not big drama queens.

One of the women on the dais addresses us. "There are many reasons each of you has come to be here today. Some of you have relatives, or spouses. Either way, you all know that this is the land where you can succeed and prosper. You've come to live the American dream and to enjoy the country's great freedom and rights. But with rights come great responsibilities."

Shouldering that great responsibility is primarily what I came here for today. Question 87 of the citizenship test is "What is the most important right granted to U.S. citizens?" The answer, *formulated by the government itself,* is "the right to vote." As we file out of the room, I ask someone who works there where the voter registration forms are. I am met with a shrug. "A church group used to hand them out but they ran out of money, I think."

I don't go to the post office to then have to buy my stamps from a bunch of Girl Scouts outside, and if the Girl Scouts are sick that day, then I'm shit out of luck. A church group? Why isn't there a form clipped to my naturalization certificate? It is difficult not to see something insidious in this oversight while standing in this sea of humanity, the majority of whom are visible minorities.

Sarah presents me with a hardbound copy of the United States Constitution and we head back to the station. We have half an hour to kill before our train. If I thought the lack of America-related decor in the main room of the citizenship facility was lousy public relations, it is as nothing compared with this port of entry: the town of Hempstead itself. Sarah and I attempt a walk around. My first glimpse as a citizen of this golden land is not the Lady of the Harbor shining her beacon through the Atlantic mist but cracked pavement, cheap liquor stores with thick Plexiglas partitions in front of the cashiers, shuttered businesses, and used car lots. The only spot of brightness on the blighted landscape is the window of the adult book and video store, with its two mannequins, one wearing a shiny stars-and-stripes bra-and-G-string set, and the other in a rainbow thong. Just like dreamy former New Jersey governor Jim McGreevey, I could comfortably dance in either of these native costumes of my twin identities.

MY FIRST INDEPENDENCE Day as an American comes scarcely two weeks later. I mark it by heading down to the nation's capital to celebrate with my old friend Madhulika, also newly American herself. Washington, D.C., is a sultry place in July. We stay indoors, hanging out and preparing a proper July Fourth meal of barbecued beer-can chicken and corn on the cob. In the evening, once the heat has broken, we head off with her husband, Jim, and their two daughters to see the fireworks. In the past, we might have lain out on the vast lawns of the Mall, but they have been fenced and cordoned off for security, so we park ourselves in a group of several hundred, sitting down on the pavement and grassy median in front of the DAR building.

The fireworks are big and bombastic and seem much louder and more aggressive than those in New York. Then again, in New York I'm usually on some rooftop miles away from the action. We are right under the explosions here. A little girl behind me, strapped into her stroller, twists in fear and panic as the percussive reports of the rockets thud through her rib cage. "No no no," she moans softly throughout the entire thirty-minute show.

She has my sympathies one hundred percent. I have made a terrible miscalculation, at least insofar as coming down to D.C. I adore my friends, and the floodlit Greek revival buildings of Capitol Hill are undeniably beautiful and a suitable representation of the majesty of this great nation of which I am now a part, but I'm not being glib when I say that one of the most compelling reasons for my having become a citizen was to entrench and make permanent my relationship with New York, the great love of my life. Being down here feels a bit like I chose to go on my honeymoon with my in-laws while my beloved waits for me back at the apartment. There is a supercomputer somewhere in the Nevada desert whose sole function is to count the number of times that I have said the following, because it is unquantifiable by human minds at this point, but this time it's really true: I should have stayed home.

THERE ARE ALREADY forty people waiting on line by seven o'clock on Election Day morning. My local polling place is in the basement of a new NYU dormitory on the corner of Four-teenth Street and Third Avenue. An ugly box of a building, it was erected on the site of the old dirty bookstore where, coin-cidentally, one could also enter booths to manipulate levers of a different sort.

It has been an awfully long time between drinks for me. I haven't voted since I was eighteen, when I cast a ballot in Canada during my first summer back from college. It's not that I take voting lightly. Quite the opposite. Living down in the United States where the coverage of Canadian politics is pretty well nonexistent, I never felt well-enough informed to have an opinion. But even if I had made it my business to stay abreast of things—going to the library to read the foreign papers in those pre-Internet years—after a certain point, I no longer felt entitled to have a say in Canada's affairs, having essentially abandoned the place. I suspect this is going to happen for the next little while every time I have to do some-thing unmistakably American, like cast a ballot in a non-parliamentary election or go through customs on my U.S. passport, but standing here on line, I am stricken with such guilt and buyer's remorse, overcome with a feeling of such nostalgia for where I came from, with its socialized medicine and gun control, that it is all I can do not to break ranks and start walking uptown and not stop until I reach the 49th parallel. There is also an equal part of me that is completely thrilled to finally be part of the electoral process. I am not alone in my exuberance this morning. Many people around me also seem filled with a buoyant and tentative excitement that George Bush might very well lose *this* election, as well. Complete strangers are talking to one another, almost giddy at the prospect. Others emerge from having voted and raise both their hands with crossed fingers, shaking them at us like maracas. "Good luck!" they wish us as they head off to work. It's almost like a party in this crowded dormitory basement that smells like a foot.

I love everything about the booth: the stiff, pleated curtain; the foursquare, early-industrial heaviness of the brass switches; the no-nonsense 1950s primary-school font of the labels; the lever that gives out a satisfying *tchnk* when I pull it back. It all feels solid and tried and tested. In the very best way, un-Floridian.

For the rest of the day I bound the floor of the apartment like a caged tiger, unable to settle. I make and receive dozens of phone calls. My in-box is full of well over a hundred e-mails from friends, all on precisely the same theme: early numbers and preliminary exit polls, predictions from the pundits, all pointing to a Kerry victory. We are contacting one another the way my immediate family obsessively did in the final days of my sister's first pregnancy leading up to the birth of my oldest nephew. We are trying to bear witness for one another in these last few moments of the never-to-be-returned-to time of Before. It's overblown and starry-eyed, we know. Even if Kerry wins, he's going to inherit some pretty insurmountable messes both here and abroad, but it is a function of what a shitty four years it has been that we still feel we are on the cusp of something potentially miraculous and life-changing.

The city that evening feels like New Year's Eve, without the menace. My neighborhood is full of people walking by with bottles of booze, on their way to watch the returns with friends; restaurants and bars have their doors open and their TVs on. Even I have no fewer than four parties to go to. I plan to skip lightly from venue to venue, until I end up somewhere, standing in a crowd of like-minded albeit younger and more attractive Democrats, just as the final polls close and they announce the new president. It will be one big booty call for justice.

That was before everything turned brown. Before the ever-reddening map rooted me to one spot. Before I parked myself at my friends' apartment, overstaying my welcome and slowly getting drunk. I eventually give up before they declare Ohio, and stagger home sometime after midnight. I turn off the alarm before I go to sleep. I don't want to hear the news in the morning. Daybreak rouses me, anyway. I lie there awake, unable to move. If I put my foot on the floor, it will make it true: four more years. I stay where I am, frozen, my bladder full. I'll have to get up soon, but for a few more minutes, I try not to waste my beautiful mind. Eventually, I turn on the radio and cold reality comes flooding in. I know of a journalist who, when Reagan was reelected, called everyone she knew—friends, acquaintances, everyone—and weepingly screamed "President Shithead! President Shithead!" into the phone. I understand the impulse, but I try to be philosophical as I start my day. He can't be president forever. Besides, I can wait him out. It's not like I'm going anywhere.

WHAT IS THE SOUND OF
ONE HAND SHOPPING?

Our waiter is looking wistful, his eyes cast downward, the merest hint of a smile playing gently upon his lips. He is about to speak. We lean forward, expecting perhaps a treasured but bittersweet memory: heedless young lovers in Paris, the specter of war looming. Instead, he begins, "There's a *really* lovely story about the calzone . . ."

This is a Temple of Food, a well-known restaurant in northern California whose owner is world famous as an advocate for humane and sustainable agribusiness, as well as being a renowned chef in her own right. I have three of her cookbooks myself. There is a sense of occasion in just being here, an awestruck thrill on the diners' faces, as if we have been chosen for something miraculous, like the people massed in the desert at the end of *Close Encounters*. Various members of the waitstaff beam at me as I walk through the dining room on my way to pee. They smile the way one might at a twelve-year-old clutching his first copy of *Catcher in the Rye,* their eyes shining with vicarious, anticipatory excitement at the journey I am about to take.

The meal is an undeniable pleasure. The food is unfussy and simply prepared, the impeccable ingredients each a Platonic example of itself: the tender micro greens of my composed salad, the piece of line-caught fish in its fragrant herbal bath. And for dessert, one medjoul date and a just-picked local tangerine, both perfect. In the same elegiac calzone tones, our waiter tells us, "We'd like to encourage you to bruise the orange leaf between your fingers." We nibble our delicious dates. As instructed, we crush the orange leaves and the airborne oils create a lovely perfume that mingles with the steam of our post-supper coffee.

Lenny Bruce described flamenco as being an art form wherein a dancer applauds his own ass. There's a lot of flamenco going around the room tonight. Smiles of mutual congratulation beam from table to table. Glasses are raised. We celebrate not only our small part in this incremental triumph over factory farming that just being here this evening represents but also our elevated capacities. It takes an exceptionally fine tongue and palate, you must admit, to appreciate a dessert of a single date. One so very different from the cratered, preservative-strafed mouths of the masses. I overhear one bartender say to the other, "I think I'm going to stay in this weekend and roast garlic." The man of a departing couple leans in and says something to his date. She listens, and gives an almost electric start. Like Warren Beatty and Diane Keaton in *Reds* who, caught up in the joyous throngs of the ten days that shook the world, had no choice after witnessing something so glorious and world-changing but to race home and fuck each other silly, the man and woman share a look of smoldering, unbridled lust. What did he whisper? "I was just told that they hadn't served that vinegar *in twenty-four years!*"

SUBTLETIES OF FLAVOR previously thought nonexistent or at the very least nonsensical are now the subject of earnest interrogation. It was easy enough to avoid such conversations—once the sole province of stultifying wine talk—by faking a coughing fit or simply bleeding from the eyes whenever your oenophile friends got going. Such discussions now cover just about anything you put into your mouth. In the food section of *The New York Times* (a newspaper which, in the interest of full disclosure, I read every day and have worked for extensively in the past), Amanda Hesser, a generally very fine journalist, writing about *fleur de sel,* had this to say about the sea salt that is harvested in France and available in New York City for $36 a kilo: "As I ate them, fine crystals of salt sprinkled on the potatoes crackled under my teeth, releasing tiny bursts that tasted of the sea and its minerals. There was no sting at the back of the mouth, no bitterness, just a silky, salty essence wrapping each bite of potato." Sting at the back of the

mouth? Bitterness? What has poor Amanda Hesser been doing all these years to add some savor to her food? Licking undeveloped Polaroids?

The general *New York Times* reader enjoys the privileges
and plentitude of life in the world's wealthiest country, so articles on rolling cigarettes out of pocket lint or recipes on sal-
vaging that last bit of rotting pork would make no sense. But
is it completely naïve to think that a squib in the same newspaper about ice cubes frozen from a river in the Scottish
Highlands and overnighted to your doorstep—the perfect
complement to your single malt—necessarily demands, if for
no other reason than to preserve some vague notion of karmic
balance, either a great big "April Fool's!" scrawled across the
top, or a prefatory note of apology that such a service even exists? Surely when we've reached the point where we're
fetishizing sodium chloride and water, and subjecting both to
the kind of scrutiny we used to reserve for choosing an oncol-
ogist, it's time to admit that the relentless questing for that
next undetectable gradation of perfection has stopped being
about the thing itself and crossed over into a realm of narcis-
sism so overwhelming as to make the act of masturbation look
selfless.

It would be peevish and ungracious after being taken to
such a lovely supper in this Temple of Food, I know, but I am
desperate to ask the question that begs to be posed: "Just how
fucking good can olive oil get?" I will stipulate to having both
French sea salt and a big bottle of extra virgin in my kitchen.
And while the presence of both might go some small distance
in pigeonholing me demographically, neither one of them

makes me a good person. They are mute and useless indicators of the content of my character.

Or at least I used to think so. Since anyone with taste buds will respond to the trans-fat bells and whistles of a hot fudge sundae or super nachos, how better then to show a nobility of spirit than by broadcasting your capacity to discern the gustatory equivalent of a hummingbird's cough as it beats its wings near a blossom that grows by a glassy pond on the other side of a distant mountain? No surer proof that one is meant for better things than an easily bruised delicacy. Such a perfectly tuned instrument can quickly suss out the cheap and nasty. So, the bitterness at the back of the throat; the polite refusal of the glass of whiskey marred by those (*shudder*) domestic ice cubes; the physical and psychic insult that are sheets of anything short of isotopic density. What is the thread count, Kenneth? We have become an army of multiply chemically sensitive, high-maintenance princesses trying to make our way through a world full of irksome peas.

There are those who might argue that the materials focused on—cotton, salt, oil, water—are themselves so basic, almost beneath notice, so much the opposite of a ski chalet in Gstaad, for example, that such epicurean monasticism is itself an act of humility by association. The temporal and vulgar rejected in favor of what really matters most in life. And what is it that matters most in life? Here's a hint: it's a pronoun that can be effectively conveyed without any words at all. Just take your index finger and point it to the center of your chest, an inch and a half from your precious, *precious* heart.

———

I TUTORED ADULT literacy at a men's shelter for about two years a while back. Have no fear, this isn't going to be one of those Capraesque anecdotes full of lachrymose inanities like "There are those who might say that I taught Tito. But if you ask me, it's *Tito* who taught *me.*" I only want to tell the following story: Christmas was coming, and Sylvia, the amazing woman who ran the career center, mentioned that a lot of the guys in the program would be going to see their kids, wives, and girlfriends, etc., for the first time since getting back on the road to recovery. All of the men had histories of drug abuse or alcoholism, a lot of them had been homeless. Their families had really gone through hell and Sylvia thought it would be nice to somehow arrange it so that the men weren't showing up empty-handed. Even a small token would go a very long way in repairing relationships that had been sorely tested over the years. I called up my friend Rory, who raided the giveaway closets of the various glossy women's magazines at which she works, eventually filling up two large boxes with fancy cosmetics and toiletries. More than enough for all the men to arrive bearing gifts.

Since the program had both a strong recovery and a Christian foundation, Sylvia went through the boxes, setting aside those things she thought might be less than suitable. Anything boozy or overtly sexual—bourbon-flavored massage oil, for example—would be out. When I looked over what she had discarded, I saw that, without exception, she had taken out the big-ticket, really expensive items.

"They're not going to understand that these are fancy

things," she said, indicating the exorbitant bottle of witch hazel with its unadorned, text-heavy label like a purgative tonic from an old dispensary, and the bar of soap resembling a rough, gray river stone wrapped up in brown paper and tied with waxed string. "They're going to think the guys got them medicine from the drugstore. It would look like the exact opposite of a present. These things just look . . . ," she searched for the word, "poor. They're already poor. Why would they want to be reminded of that?"

Clearly Sylvia and the men of the mission had no appreciation for the soul-cleansing charms of Kiehl's blue astringent. It's also a safe bet, given the mission's cafeteria-style dining hall, that the austere and rustic appeal of Le Pain Quotidien— a small chain of restaurants in the city where you can enjoy your salade niçoise sitting at a long unvarnished table beside your fellow New Yorkers as if you had all just come in from re-seeding the north forty—would also be lost on them. What would they make of other such high-end examples of com-modified faux poverty, like Republic Noodles, which looks like a Chinese Cultural Revolution–era reeducation facility. For models.

Or the wallpaper from Scalamandré called the Rogar-shevsky Scroll, named after the family who occupied one of the apartments in the building that now houses New York's Lower East Side Tenement Museum? The design is a faithful copy of the fourteenth layer of paper found when they reno-vated. A pretty floral pattern, it must have put up a valiant fight against the grime and cold-water squalor of the place. It's nice to think that those Rogarshevskys fortunate enough not to have had to pitch themselves out of burning shirtwaist factory windows were cheered by the sight of it when they returned from their fifteen-hour piecework shifts. Might an immigrant family employed in one of Manhattan's sweatshops that still exist today have access to the same visual solace? Not likely. The Rogarshevsky Scroll is available to the trade for upward of $80 a roll. And how about the armchair designed by Brazilian brothers Huberto and Fernando Campana out of a seemingly random assemblage of hundreds of pieces of wooden lath? The ingenious and counterintuitively comfortable chair is called the Favela, named for the jury-rigged, destitute, crime-ridden shantytowns that climb the hillsides of Rio de Janeiro. According to the International Finance Corporation, a public policy organization associated with the World Bank, the average monthly income for a family in the Brazilian favelas is two hundred reais, or roughly $72. The Favela armchair retails for over $3,000.

Oh Sylvia, I want to say, *don't you know that if you curl your lip enough, you can make "poor" sound just like "pure"?*

It's nice to have nice things. Creature comfort is not some bourgeois capitalist construct, but framing it as a moral virtue sure is. It's what the French call *Nostalgie de la Boue*: a fond yearning for the mud. Two things have to be in place to really appreciate this particular brand of gluttony posing as asceticism. First, you have to have endured years and years of plenty, the mud a long-distant, nearly forgotten memory. One must have decades of such surfeit under your belt that you have been fortunate enough to grow sick of it all. (Using this economic model, Russians thirty years hence might pose less of a threat to the imperiled world supply of Versace and sequins.) And second—and this is what really separates the men from the boys—in order to maintain a life free of clutter and suitable for a sacred space, you'll need another room to hide your shit.

And it is shit, ultimately. Or some corporeal, effluvial cousin thereof. This sloughing off and scouring down to the walls is about a denial that has little to do with doing without. It is not so much the forgoing of one's fleshly desires as much as a terrified repudiation of the essential nature of what we are: great sloshing, suppurating bags of wet, prone to rupture. Mortal messes just waiting to happen.

And who wants to be reminded of that? An apocryphal story attributed to Diana Vreeland tells of a young woman working as an editor who is done dirt by her man, who turns out to be a crumb, so she throws herself in front of the rush hour IRT. She sustains only minor physical injuries and is packed off to some place like Payne Whitney or Austen Riggs where she can get better. Returning to her job months later, repaired but shaky, she is called into Mrs. Vreeland's office. The arbitrix of style rises from her chair and taking the wounded bird's hands in both of hers, says consolingly, "My dear, here at *Vogue* we don't throw ourselves in front of trains. If we must, we take pills."

THE COURT OF Heian Japan, which existed a thousand years ago, was a society of exquisite indolence. Nobles might spend hours choosing the perfect shade of silk underrobe, barely an inch of which would be glimpsed from the gaping sleeve of a kimono. Days passed in splendid idleness playing arcane word games where one had to match the first half of an ancient Chinese epigram written on one clamshell with the second half written on another (yahoo!). Hours were taken up composing erudite mash notes to one's lover of the moment. Sei Shonagon, a lady of the court, kept a "pillow book," a compendium of her rarefied observations and impressions. It is an amazing volume, covering a wide range of topics, about all of which she had very strong opinions. Although it was written a millennium ago, its frequent blazing triviality and tone of aphoristic certitude on matters aesthetic can make it seem eerily contemporary and magazine-ready: "These are the months that I like best: The First Month, the Third, the Fourth, the Fifth, The Seventh, the Eighth, The Ninth, The Eleventh, and the Twelfth." "Oxen should have very small foreheads . . ." "Things That Should Be Large: Priests. Fruit. Houses." And this entry from Unsuitable Things: "Snow on the houses of common people. This is especially regrettable when the moonlight shines down on it." Simplicity, it seems, has always been wasted on those who simply cannot appreciate it.

SESIÓN PRIVADA

C lose one eye and block out the stand of tattered palms with your thumb, and the tiny San Pedro airport, battered by horizontal sheets of rain, has some of the gray, hardscrabble charm of the Scottish coast. But unless you are featuring the gray, hardscrabble charms of the Girls of the Scottish Coast, this is about the last thing you want for a *Playboy* shoot. You certainly don't send a still photographer, videographer and crew, and three centerfolds to equatorial Belize looking for weather like this. And *Sesión Privada*, the Latin American Playboy TV program that is due to start shooting the next day, is at least partly about weather. In addition to featuring "the unrivaled beauty and sensuality of Latin and

Brazilian women," the show also highlights some of the prime tourist destinations of our neighbors to the south. *Sesión Privada* is a combination of lingering views of nude female flesh interspersed with slow pans of the Caribbean landscape. Apparently those shots of white sand, lapping waves, and swaying palm trees all provide some necessary downtime for the average viewer. According to the producer, men can look at naked women for just so long. This is news to me. I don't mean that snidely, it is simply news to me. I don't look at naked women.

Past *Sesións* have been filmed in places like Fortaleza, Brazil, and Tobago. This episode will be shot on Cayo Espanto, an exclusive resort off the Belize barrier reef. Cayo Espanto is a private island with just five secluded villas, each of which goes for about $1,300 a night. Guests range from the merely filthy rich to the seriously affluent: sports-team owners, friends of the George and Barbara Bushes, and the like.

Any unfettered display of hedonism is on hold until the stormy lowering skies clear up. So far, only the photographer and I have made it. The three lucky women who will be featured, the winner and two runners-up of a *Playboy* beauty contest held the previous night in Acapulco, have yet to arrive. The photographer is an almost ridiculously handsome Finn— tan skin, silver-blond hair, and ice-blue eyes. He resembles one of those cyborgs from the movies, developed in a secret mountain enclave laboratory who, as his wrappings are taken off, is introduced by the evil genius who created him with a portentous "Gentlemen, may I present, the Perfect Killing Machine!"

We are escorted to the nearby San Pedro boat slip by one of Cayo Espanto's staff, who radios ahead with our drink orders. The downpour has turned the town of San Pedro into a bog of muddy destitution. Or at least a very good imitation of it. I am assured repeatedly that what I am seeing is not abject poverty so much as the aftermath of the devastation of Hurricane Keith, which blew through in October 2000. The improvised, ramshackle nature of the town is only the result of the houses that were reassembled from the salvaged lumber.

By contrast, Cayo Espanto, a five-minute boat ride across not unpleasantly sulfur-scented water, is a scant three acres of immaculately raked white sand and evenly spaced palm trees. It is a serene and lovely antidote to the debris-strewn urbanity of San Pedro. That I should feel such relief calls up its own uneasiness, which is only amplified by the eight staff members who have come to greet our arrival. They might easily take shelter from the rain under one of the two palm-thatched *palapas* at the end of the dock, but are instead obediently lined up in the drizzle like the von Trapp children being disciplined. The long dock is edged on both sides with conch shells, their furled pink openings facing out. Appropriate for the weekend photo shoot, like a landing strip at Georgia O'Keeffe International Airport. Incoming vaginas!

A young man holds an umbrella over my head and escorts me to my villa, the Casa Olita, or Little Wave House. This is Obed, my personal houseman. Obed will spend the next twenty-four hours at my beck and call, announcing his presence with a dulcet "hello" a deferential ten feet from the louvered doors of my private house.

Let me say that Cayo Espanto is really beautiful and everyone with whom I came in contact there was endlessly solicitous and very nice. A few days prior to my arrival, I had been sent a three-page questionnaire about my likes and dislikes in food, bedding, activities, do I prefer to be spoiled with attention or to be left alone, etc. If you have a large gunnysack of disposable income and you are looking for pampering and relaxation, you simply cannot find a better place than this tropical paradise.

It's just that I am not big on pampering and relaxation. I can't help feeling that the world's laziest coal miner is probably in greater need of a vacation like this than the most dogged CEO. As for myself, I haven't put in anything resembling an honest day's work in years so I am uncomfortable, to say the least, with being given a servant.

The playmates arrive later in the afternoon. I walk down to the dock to greet them, taking my place in line with the staff. The girls have no idea who I am, but as I am the only one holding a notebook and not wearing a uniform, all three ladies see fit to kiss me hello on both cheeks. We have no real common language so they settle on telling me just their names and countries of origin. They are Alejandra from Venezuela, the contest winner, and her two runners up: Vanessa from Argentina, and from Brazil, Patricia, or Patty for short, which in her own liquid-mouthed pronunciation of it sounds like the word "party" said by a lugubrious Brit. They are very sweet and seem quite pretty, but at twenty-three, twenty-three, and twenty-one years of age, respectively, and not yet sporting their *Playboy* makeup, they also seem ridiculously young. Exhausted from their long trip, they go off to bed, leaving me behind to have my full Cayo Espanto experience.

An experience best shared by two, it must be said. Everything is designed for coupled isolation here: the pair of teak deck chairs at the end of my long private dock, the intimate dining table at the foot of my king-size bed. The five villas of the island are invisible one from the other. The reality TV show *Temptation Island* filmed its "dream date" sequence on Cayo Espanto for a reason.

But I am not on a dream date, indeed as I almost never am. Rather, I am Charles Foster Kane in the final reel, standing by myself looking out at the ocean from beside my personal splash pool. My very good supper is a meal for one, eaten while staring out at the black sea. At one point, in the palmy shadows just off of my veranda, a man in full mariachi regalia plays guitar and sings two plaintive songs just for me. I don't speak Spanish, but I'm pretty sure the chorus of one of them is, "David, you will die alone." The mosquito netting is prepared around my bed and I retire, the aging tycoon lulled to sleep by the rhythmic pumping, pumping of his oil wells.

I wake at sunrise with my usual need to pee that graduates to desperate as I try to find my way out from under the mosquito netting, a ninety-second procedure to untangle myself from what must conservatively be forty yards of fabric. The rain is gone and the day has dawned cloudless and blue, the ocean an expanse of celadon. It is *Playboy* weather. At only 8:00 a.m., the sun is already beating down like a bell clapper and the temperature is climbing steadily. I make my way a hundred yards across the sand over to where the girls are staying.

All is happy industry here at the Casa Aurora (House of the Rising Sun, *heh heh*). The ladies have made themselves at home. Clearly someone is studying English, but it seems like the classic Playmate stereotype when I spy the two books on the small coffee table: *Pinocchio and the Whale* and *I Love Boats!* The music blares, Vanessa is tanning and doing her nails on the deck, Patty is having her hair done. Alejandra is going through possible outfits with the producer and photographer. The entire wardrobe for a two-day shoot involving three women could fit into your average dopp kit. The bed is a flimsy profusion of marabou-trimmed panties, bras, and see-through tops.

Alejandra is included in the deliberations as she tries on various ensembles. "This is it?" she asks, rather disappointed in the cream thong and sheer cream crop top. "It's too simple." She's right, actually. Even I can see that there is something a little austere and athletic about the getup. More J. Crew than *Playboy*. Finally settling on a black thong and a bra with looping arcs of hanging jet beads, Alejandra looks like a Victorian lampshade. A Victorian lampshade with enormous knockers. Impressive rack notwithstanding, however, Alejandra has the virtually hairless, slim-hipped build of a twelve-year-old boy.

Thoughts of twelve-year-old boys aren't really out of place. Their hormonal spirit is the guiding aesthetic force behind *Sesión Privada*. The show is predicated on that horny preteen-male belief that, even better than seeing a naked woman, *being* a naked woman would be the best thing in the whole world. One's *privada* moments would involve little more than standing in front of a mirror, gazing at the intoxicating proximity of your hot, nude, nude, totally nude lady self.

Patty is the first to demonstrate, as she stands wearing a see-through top and thong in the striped sunlight on the deck of a villa, undulating pre-orgasmically to no apparent stimulus. She looks into the camera, her beryl-green eyes closed to fiery slits. There is no come-hither in her gaze. No one else need ever show up. Holding on, Samson-like, to the louvered doors, she arches her back and throws her blond mane.

"Ah, the *Playboy* hair toss. Never seen *that* before," says the producer.

I take refuge in the shade. Obed appears with an iced towel for me to put against the back of my neck. Small lizards skitter back and forth while a hermit crab makes achingly slow progress across the sand. I strike up a conversation with the hair-and-makeup guy. He tells me about the competition these women have won. It was just a garden-variety beauty contest with one glaring difference.

"Okay," he murmurs conspiratorially, pitching his voice somewhat lower and leaning in, "these are not girls from the United States. They don't wax, they don't tweeze, they don't pluck. I was *exhausted*."

In truth, I'm not sure that bushier eyebrows or unmodified treasure trails would have changed anything, really. Hairy or smooth, the antics are fairly banal. It's a pretty uncomplex transaction.

Vanessa's pictorial is still more writhing, only this time on the bed under the billowing mosquito netting. The director stops her and she takes five, relaxing in her last position, on her knees and elbows. It looks more medical than erotic. The crew confers about her moves. The video-camera man demonstrates what they want. Sinking to his knees, he twists his torso and drags his open palms slowly up his chest to his head where they rub slow circles through a hypothetical jungle of tousled hair. Vanessa laughs and beckons him onto the bed to do it for the camera. Perhaps this is just the nature of softcore, but the girls' hands are kept so primly far away from their genitals that all of their crypto-masturbatory back arching and moaning for no apparent reason starts to look a little mentally unbalanced, frankly. Unless, of course, it's actually the appointments of this private villa that's doing it for them, although I doubt it. While I have known people who do get a little moist over high-quality linens or superior window treatments, they are not, in a word, women.

By 2:00, I am as desperate as Dustin Hoffman in *Papillon* to escape the island. I am not built for this heat and sunlight, and truth be told, I am a little bored. I had thought that this experience would be an eye-opener, would provide me with lots of new information. As a homosexual delivered by cesarean section, I have spent my life at a double remove. But

images like the ones playing out in front of me are so ubiquitous, so much a part of every deodorant ad and bra commercial, that there are no real surprises here.

I procure a boat ride over to San Pedro. Germán, the man
who drives me, takes the aquatic equivalent of backroads to
town, winding the boat through narrow channels overgrown
with snarls of mangrove trees on either side. We pass by modest houses on stilts, ingenious patchwork constructions of
mismatched materials. An entire family, from grandparents to
infants, are enjoying the sunny weather by swimming in the
water in front of their house, an abandoned refrigerator cheerfully bobbing in the water beside them. They wave hello as we
go by.

I will be picked up and returned to Cayo Espanto in time
for supper. I walk the main drag. A hurricane can do a lot to a
place, granted, but last I checked, it cannot rip the macadam
off a road. Small trucks drive by, as well as a number of golf
carts, the latter invariably driven by white vacationers. There
are shops selling lighters, T-shirts, some carvings. Apparently
there is a vibrant nightlife where tourists make their pub
crawls from plywood bar to plywood bar. As I pass a garbage
can, an iguana suddenly rears up out of it and motionlessly regards me.

Everywhere I go, be it the airport in Belize City or the small
shops of San Pedro, everyone I speak to keeps on assuring me
how happy Belizians are. In a "Dos and Don'ts" tourist pam-
phlet I pick up, I am told to go out and enjoy the town; that
the San Pedranos are extremely pleased that I am there. I

hope that's the case, that happiness does reign here. I encounter nothing but smiling faces. But the repeated insistence
of this monolithic pronouncement about their national character makes it seem suspect.

Just before 6:00, making my way back to the debris-strewn
jetty, a local man whom I have never met stops me in the
street to tell me Germán and my boat are waiting. I am known
after having been in town for all of four hours. We skim along
the water back to the private island, the mariachi from the
night before sitting beside me, already wearing his bedizened
costume.

THE SUN GOES down giving way to a clear Caribbean night
awash in stars. Belize apparently sits just underneath the path
of many satellites. We can see them skittering back and forth
across the sky. A group dinner has been set up outside, underneath an enormous umbrella of palm fronds. The chef is roast-
ing an entire pig in a covered pit. Occasional wisps of smoke
curl up through the sand, like vain attempts at escape by the
spirit of the butchered animal.

The crew toasts one another and the models on a day's work
well done. The mariachi plays. Alejandra calls over to him and
makes a request. She laughs a little as she says the name of
the song, half joking. Even though she asks him in Spanish,
the ironic, camp lilt in her voice is unmistakable. He begins to
sing. It is a sweetly traditional tune, a song a mother might
teach her child. As he begins, Alejandra and Vanessa laugh
and exclaim in mock-sentimentality. But they cannot sustain

the joke, and soon they just sit and listen, eyes cast down, with faint smiles on their faces.

This is my classic trajectory: the midafternoon freak-out followed by that evening's outflowing of fine feeling, brought on by a number of factors: relief at my impending departure, a drop in temperature, and the very tangible perquisites heaped upon me—good food, alcohol, and the general deference accorded an American journalist abroad. I have been having a little *sesión privada* of my own. My version of the extended cock tease is that throughout my short stay on Cayo Espanto I have been affecting either a wide-eyed, disingenuous unfamiliarity with luxury, or, alternately, claiming outrage at the social inequities of the place. Whenever Obed has asked me if I'd like something, I have responded with a scandalized, "Oh golly, no! Thank you so much, though," horrified that he might think I would want anything, only to have him then bring me the drink, the chair, the umbrella anyway, and then I, uttering a sheepish and humiliated "thank you," drink, sit, take the shade. Every single time. I am suffused with well-being and just as quickly sickened with myself. Mine are the tears of the Walrus, bemoaning the wholesale carnage of his little oyster friends as he scoops another bivalve into his voracious, sucking maw.

THE FOLLOWING AFTERNOON, back at the San Pedro airport, I wait to board the small eight-seat plane—a boxy little number with some unsettling rusty spots, and the completely terrifying airline logo on its tail fin of a man (our pilot?)

flat-out asleep under a palm tree with his hat over his eyes. I watch the baggage handler as he stuffs our luggage into the bottom of the fuselage. A leathery man in his fifties, he wears a tight, faded yellow T-shirt with Daffy Duck on it. Daffy is staggering, his drunken path indicated by a dashed, serpentine line. Beside him are the words "I was Loony as a Toon at Samantha's Bat Mitzvah."

It would be nice to think that this T-shirt was his from the start, that he *was* at Samantha's bat mitzvah, sharing in her family's joy as she came into Jewish womanhood, and came away with this souvenir of his time there. But, much like the consoling fiction of a private island where three beautiful goddesses wait, trembling and naked beneath the mosquito netting for someone, *anyone,* to come and satisfy their burning, unquenchable desire, I kind of doubt it.

WILDMAN

A flower grows in Brooklyn. The tiny chamomile blossom
has pushed its way through a crack in the gray pavement. Before I can come up with a hackneyed metaphor for
its patient and valiant struggle toward the light, "Wildman"
Steve Brill—edible-plant expert, vegan cookbook author, and
"New York's best-known naturalist"—bends down and summarily picks the small domed bud to point out to us the plant's
physical characteristics. Advantage asphalt.

This mini-lecture seems more a gentle attempt to sell us
the small magnifying loupes Brill has available for $10 than to
impart any truly useful botanical knowledge. The real information will come once we walk through the gates of Prospect

Park, Brooklyn's 526-acre wilderness. There, we will learn all about how to identify and forage our own wild edibles.

Left with some time to kill as our group assembles, Brill entertains our youngest member, two-year-old Adeline, with "Pop Goes the Weasel," played by clapping his cupped hands in front of his open mouth. By changing the shape of his lips, he is able to create a surprisingly supple instrument that can play an impressive range of notes. The whole range of notes, in fact. Brill does not stint on the length of his version. As he moves out of the minor-key bridge back to the initial verse, Addie's attention has shifted. Then again, so has Brill's. His clap-mouth has put him into a minor fugue state. With his eyes now focused upward with an expression both dreamy and vacant, he appears almost saintlike. Or would, if not for his Intrepid Explorer drag of wicker pith helmet and cargo pants.

One of our group, a teacher from upstate New York, addresses Brill as "Wildman," with the respectful deference of an acolyte and no trace of irony. Brill, in turn, sees nothing odd in the honorific. This man is waiting for a fellow teacher, a cybernetic pen pal from an online Christian prayer forum. They have chosen this expedition for their first face-to-face meeting. It's unclear if it's a date or not, although she'd be well served if it wasn't because, unbidden, he tells us, "I had a friend in college who caught an albino squirrel, and mistreated it so badly that the animal eventually retaliated, and bit him really, really deep right here," he says, indicating the fleshy pad at the base of his thumb. "The squirrel wouldn't let go until my friend broke its neck." There is no way to tell what this man thinks about his anecdote. His tone is almost completely uninflected, holding neither outrage nor humor.

Also in our search party is a venture capitalist who runs a nonprofit theater program for inner city youth in Newark. He has completed numerous wilderness survival courses. There is a Deborah Harry type, her hair bleached to the color and consistency of dry straw, her eyelids shaded with pink to offset her pink rhinestone cat's-eye glasses. She is here as part of her day job, which is assisting in cooking classes at New York's Natural Gourmet Cookery School. With her is her boyfriend from Mexico, whose head is wrapped in an American eagle scarf and whose T-shirt reads "Gateways of Annihilation." Just twelve people out for a Sunday afternoon of diversion in a lovely city park. We're almost a Seurat painting.

We have followed the instructions we got from Brill when we signed up, and have arrived with packed lunches, plastic bags for our eventual hauls of free comestibles (as well as air-permeable paper sacks for any mushrooms we might harvest), scissors for snipping, and small garden spades for digging. We have read and signed the consent form absolving Brill of any liability should we become sick, injured, or die outright from anything we might mistakenly eat, and now we are ready. "Walk this way!" Brill cries, and he's off, John Cleesing across Grand Army Plaza and into the park.

We take leave of the path almost immediately, scrambling up a hill to find our first edible, hedge mustard, a ground cover which grows plentifully and has been alleged to inhibit both ovarian and prostate cancers. I eat some. It tastes . . . green. One of the overriding flavors of the day will be chlorophyll.

Brill is a combination of great knowledgeability and relentless borscht belt schtickiness. Identifying a sample as having a tooth-edged leaf, he drops it with an exaggerated gesture and yells at the plant, "Stop biting me!" We are advised not to spill the seeds of our garlic mustard: "Particularly if you're Catholic, you should never spill your seeds."

Prospect Park is vast. A once carefully controlled design by landscape architect Frederick Law Olmsted that was meant to serve as a benevolent antidote to the rough justice of "real" nature, it has grown during its century-plus life and now contains a variety of terrains and mini-ecosystems. In a formal English garden, we eat dainty violet leaves. Moving farther into a forested area, we munch on the parsley-tasting leaves of the goutweed, named not for the disease but for a bastardization of "goat," its primary consumer. Coincidentally, chickweed, which we sample next—and which tastes of corncobs but curiously not of corn—is also named for the animal that historically liked it best. By now, we are fully enclosed in wooded underbrush. We pass by many men, alone and in pairs, who don't appear supremely enchanted by our presence—a coed dozen, including two toddlers, led by a chattering guide dressed like Dr. Livingston. Brill, for his part, seems oblivious to this, and to the obvious grass stains on the knees of the men who walk by. It's in his own best interest to live and let live. The parks department unofficially condones what Brill does, although individual rangers may not, so we are advised to be discreet in our locustlike behavior. Every one of us here is up to something a little shady, which is as it should be. Brill began the tour by telling us that flowers were once thought to have no purpose greater than pleasing the human eye. It wasn't until experiments in pollination during the Renaissance that people realized to their puritanical horror that even the loveliest of blooms were nothing more than sex organs. In Catholic Europe, people burned Carl Linnaeus's books as corrupting filth. (To give them their due, much like the East German paranoid who is convinced that he is under surveillance by his neighbors, they kind of had a point: Linneaus *was* a bit of a sexual obsessive, vaginally fixated, pushing his penchant so far as to name an entire genus of plants *Clitoria*.) So who can blame the human fauna in this Brooklyn cruising ground for pulsing in concert with all this throbbing flora around us? It seems we can even hear it coming up through the ground itself, a muffled cellophane crackle underfoot. O, how the heart leaps when the condom wrappers are in bloom once more!

GIVEN THEIR EXPENSIVE gourmet pedigree, the hit-or-miss nature of their growth, and the fact that they are the plant world's closest thing in flavor and texture to meat, mushrooms are the big-ticket items of any wild edible foraging. We hit paydirt when we come upon some wine-cap *Stropharia*. Apparently they are delicious. Brill tells us he has made a big model of one out of clay. In fact, Brill has painted, photographed, or sculpted almost every wild mushroom there is.

On his website there is a photo of him entitled "Wildman Devours Yellow Morel Sculpture." The larger-than-life-sized replica of the torpedo-shaped fruiting body is poised at Brill's happy, open mouth, his face a display of high exuberance. It is, as Freud might say, an interesting photo. Throw another Linnaeus book on the fire, boys.

But we must be careful. The mycological kingdom abounds with treachery and deceit. Many harmless, yummy fungi have sinister false cognates—evil twins that look almost exactly the same but for some small, critical difference, much like the world of soap operas. Eat one and it will shut your liver down before you've gotten through a forkful of that omelet. I am suddenly less than certain that I have picked wine-caps and not the slender-stemmed poisonous mushrooms that were growing nearby that Brill warned us about. I give mine away to Deborah Harry, who seems only too happy to have them.

In fact, my bag is notably less full than my cohorts'. In the mere seconds between the time Brill identifies a plant and I bend down to pick some for myself, I get confused. Tops of plants can be different in form from their lower growth. Mature plants can look nothing like their juvenile selves. Even the same plant can go from edible in one form to toxic in another. And frankly, all the plants just look like leaves to me. What had initially seemed a bounteous windfall, free for the taking and free of consequence, becomes fraught with peril in short order. Pokeweed, for example, requires three separate boilings to rid it of its toxins. Brill, a vegan since 1990, has the religion and uses superlatives freely, but about pokeweed's flavor he is unstinting. Again, I give mine away. I forget how many times I have to boil it as soon as the words leave his mouth. And it seems like an awful lot of work for a potentially lethal meal.

Wildman reassures me. "Except for getting killed or sick, I've made all the foraging mistakes you can." I can't imagine what other foraging mistakes he's talking about aside from those two, and I don't know that I will be so lucky as to avoid either of them. There have always been the necessary casualties in our species' evolutionary march toward progress: the curious fool who stands out in the field to watch the electrical storm; the Neanderthal with the head cold who cannot smell enough to know that he has just eaten a very bad mussel; or, in my case, the recreational scrounger who, like the most primitive of creatures, is completely drawn in by the lovely butter-bloomed lesser celandine bush. I just want to dive in and suck the saffron-colored sap that flows from its cut stems. I want to eat all its inviting yellowness. Brill stops me. "It's like my ex-girlfriend," he cracks. "Beautiful but deadly!"

WE STOP FOR lunch under the canopy of a large spreading tree. Softball games and Ultimate Frisbee are being played out on the huge lawn. In the distance, a procession of children with large white paper crane puppets on long sticks makes its way along the crest of a hill with a strangely funereal grace. Brill gives us all a taste of his garlic mustard pesto and vegan redbud ice cream. Others have brought similarly painstakingly prepared food; there is more than one sprouted wheatberry salad in the bunch. Deborah Harry is justifiably proud of her strawberry-rhubarb agar-agar mousse. I figure it's probably best not to offer either my roast beef sandwich or Mint Milanos around for tastes. I ask Brill to tell me about himself.

He starts at the very beginning. "I'm fifty-four years old. Born on March 10, the same as Bix Beiderbecke." I'm a fan of the jazz trumpeter and I tell Brill so. He immediately clap-mouths both "In a Mist" and "Mississippi Mud" from start to finish. I eat my sandwich throughout this floor show.

Brill's present career began in 1986, when he was apprehended for eating a dandelion in New York's Central Park. The media attention paid to his misdemeanor was huge—he was on *David Letterman* and interviewed by Dan Rather for the evening news.

"I used to think that the most exciting thing that would ever happen to me in Central Park was getting arrested, but five years ago, I was leading a singles' group and met a woman who was even wilder than I am." (Brill is an eccentric, of that there is no doubt. And for all I know, his body underneath what looks to be a flame-retardant wardrobe might be covered in urban primitive tattoos and perforated with all manner of piercings, but outwardly, unless "wild" became synonymous with "Chess Club" when I wasn't paying attention, it is not the word that springs to mind when looking at him.) "We married last June . . ." he says, and claps out Mendelssohn's wedding march. "And this coming December . . ." He launches into "Rock-a-Bye Baby."

With a child on the way, Brill will have to work even harder and he is already a very busy man. He barely gets a day off during the ten months of the year the weather permits him to lead these walking tours. It's not clear what kind of a living Brill makes, but it can't be a lot. The fee today is less than $20 a person. Prior to his current career, Brill had tried to make a go of it as a vegan caterer. Before that, his ambition was to be, you guessed it, a chessmaster. At least his present job provides him with most of his food so he can use his earnings for other necessities.

The conclusion of the tour is signaled with the flourish of the Merry Melodies theme (in clap-mouth, of course) and a friendly "B-dee, B-dee, B-dee, That's All Folks!" He takes a moment to say good-bye to each of us and also manages to sell one of his books.

"Who should I sign it to? It's more valuable if I sign it," he says.

"Sign it 'To the plant world,'" says the young venture capitalist.

Brill does, and hands it over. The failure in logic in this exchange is not so much that the plant world, although living, is categorically incapable of appreciating an inscribed first edition but that even if it could, the plant world might not take too kindly to the volume in question, *The Wild Vegetarian Cookbook*.

LATER THAT NIGHT, I stand over my sink eating my salad of hedge mustard, goutweed, peppercress, and chickweed. Brill advised us to eat small amounts of anything we pick the first time out. He wasn't kidding. This is a very small but formidable bowl of food. Commercial plants are bred to be bigger and heavier. They contain more water while wild edibles contain more nutrients. I get fuller much faster than normal. There is almost too much flavor here, and a tongue-swelling rawness. It's not unpleasant, but there is a tenacity to these greens. It takes some major mastication to tear through them.

At first blush it had seemed puzzling, inconceivable almost, that the bushes of the park weren't overrun with people harvesting all of these marvelous free eats. But Brill's tour ultimately proves the opposite point. Even here we remain subordinate to the caprice of nature. At a Japanese knotweed plant, Brill finds only two eight-inch-long edible stalks left to feed twelve of us. Its season is almost over. It's wonderfully lemony, and I'm even a little full at this point, having sampled cattails, poor man's pepper, and field pennycress, but I need no clearer explication than this, standing here chewing on my meager ration no bigger than a cocktail gherkin, to see why our ancestors decided to give this up and begin growing their food.

Brill described getting arrested that day as the best thing that ever happened to him. It allowed him to forage full time, he says. But "allowed" is hardly the word I'd use. If Brill and his family are to stay alive, he is going to have to forage full time. Brill is trying to embody—and to sell to us, if only over the course of the afternoon—a lifestyle that was found to be impractical and unsustainable ten thousand years ago. As for those people on the globe still unfortunate enough to have to rely upon this method for getting their food, they definitely aren't vegans. Or if they are, it's not by choice. I would bet cash money that, if dropped down into Prospect Park, they would forgo the pokeweed, however plentiful, and the rare mushrooms, however delicious, and make a beeline over to the easily accessed protein of the hot-dog cart a hundred yards away. Even Brill, for all his obvious knowledge, industry, and sheer love for what he does, concedes this point in a way when I ask him if he ever has to shop for ingredients.

"Occasionally," he says. "I haven't seen too many tofu trees."

All of human civilization—from the first agrarian settlements at Jericho, all the way up to now—in that simple statement. Wildman heads toward the subway.

AS IT IS IN HEAVEN

The takeoff is intense, so the rumor goes. A filling-loosening interval of judder and roar, our ascent as steep as a rocket. The interior is cramped. As we approach Mach speed, we will lurch forward twice, the sonic boom will be an audible thud. At cruising altitude, almost eleven miles above the earth, I will see the curvature of the globe below, and above me, the dark blue of the stratosphere, the very edge of the black vastness of outer space. Also, a spontaneously occurring red streak runs along the ceiling, some kind of inter-cabin mini–aurora borealis electrical thingie, apparently. There is the smell of burning fuel and metal throughout the flight, I will receive a present—a pen, a silver picture frame, something like that—the food will be magnificent, and the landing will be abrupt and snap me forward in my seat.

It's like gleaning one's sex education from a group of eleven-year-old boys. Some of the information will turn out to be true-ish, some of it completely spurious. Not surprising, given the fact that, at upward of $13,800 for a round-trip ticket, those with firsthand knowledge of the Concorde are a small-ish population. I have been offered a seat on one of the final voyages and now, two days before my own Concorde trip, my head is filled with thoughts of the aircraft's twenty years of metal fatigue causing a hairline fissure that lets in super-heated air that roasts us all alive.

Jon, a friend, mentions how he flew on it when it almost crashed. I beg him not to tell me the story. "Oh, but it's one of my most charming anecdotes," he counters, and gaily launches in. Apparently, just as they were reaching Mach 2, they experienced a sudden loss of velocity. The fellow seated behind him (a civilian, as opposed to the fellow to Jon's immediate right, who was Keith Richards) leaned around and said not unexcit-edly that this had happened before and last time everyone was given a £500 gift certificate to Marks and Spencer. As they were turning the plane around and heading back to London, the co-pilot emerged from the flight deck to talk to the passen-gers. When he was reassuring Jon directly, his backseat neigh-bor leaned forward and whispered, "Ask about the vouchers." In the end none were forthcoming, leaving the passengers with nothing but their lives to console themselves for the incon-venience.

My worries are assuaged somewhat by the thought that the very rich would no sooner climb into a death trap any more willingly than the rest of us. The Concorde is hardly the un-ballasted, top-heavy ferry across the river, the rickety wooden roller coaster whose pilings have been eaten through by ter-mites, or the subterranean nightclub with no fire exits packed with young revelers smoking cigarettes and standing waist high in flammable Styrofoam packing peanuts. Except, of course, when it is, viz the chartered Concorde that caught fire and crashed within minutes of takeoff, killing everyone on board. It was because of some errant sharp metal object on the runway that wasn't supposed to be there, but still . . .

The specter of mortality that hounded me floats away when I enter the first-class lounge at Heathrow. The place is packed to the rafters and the air is musical with clinking glassware and the collective seal bark of good fortune, a peristaltic guf-faw that happens when simultaneously quaffing champagne and tossing hors d'oeuvres into laughing mouths. It is June 2003, but it might as well be Paris before the Germans marched in, so penetrating is the whiff of memory in the mak-ing, the glow of an era about to end. Air France flew its last su-personic flight a month prior, and British Airways will put its Concorde out of service forever in October.

I'd join in on the bacchanal, but my ticket is a special cheap rate (£500, coincidentally the same amount as the mythical sorry-we-almost-killed-you consolation voucher) so my seat is by no means guaranteed should someone walk up who is able to pay full fare. My presence is probationary and second class.

I feel like Lily Bart in *The House of Mirth,* who has to augment her weekend invitation to Tuxedo by doing private secretarial work for the hostess. Any minute now and I'll be asked to serve drinks. I kill some time in a carrel in the business center and check my e-mail. Opposite me is an American man on a cell phone. Midfifties, sleek ponytail, thin-soled loafers, the gold buckle of his belt half hidden beneath the gentle spillover of his well-fed, Merino-coddled belly, he has been oiled soft with wealth. He could also be an audience plant, there to reinforce the lounge's sense of exclusivity, so very Aaron Spelling is his conversation with his architect as he wonders aloud in a public voice where they might put the new entertainment/media room, gym, *and* movie theater in the remodeling of his home. He suggests, "Maybe near the stairs, where the waterfall is now."

A proper, tweedy, white-haired chap walks over and asks us if one can get online at these computers. Yes, I say, although they're dial-up connections so it might take a while. The man on the phone interrupts his conversation to agree. "Yeah, they're slow as shit," he says. The older fellow rears back ever so slightly, as if our friend has actually just taken one. Trying to dissociate myself, I retire to the smoking lounge where I run into Ponytail's travel companion, a perma-tan big shot with a silver pompadour and pornographer's goatee, heavy gold-link jewelry, chino shorts, and blinding white sneakers. He saunters in and lights up a cigarillo, despite the numerous signs requesting that we limit our tobacco consumption to cigarettes. Without asking, he changes the channel on the flat-screen television to a golf tournament. He paces the floor with a swagger of entitlement, somehow managing to take up more space than he physically occupies, and yells at the set, "Low side! Pussy side! No balls!"

As various subsonic destinations are announced, it is the older and better dressed among us who get up to leave, winnowing our ranks down to a rather normal-seeming group. There are no visibly famous people that I can see, and nearly every conversation I overhear is between people who have either upgraded, cashed in miles, or blown a wad of savings to fulfill a long-standing dream of finally being here. When the aircraft finally arrives at the gate, there is much excitement and picture snapping. The Concorde really is as beautiful as a heron: sleek, immaculate, very white, and needle-nosed.

I had been expecting some of that same *Clockwork Orange* brightness inside, but the cabin is low-ceilinged with small windows. The seats are dark blue leather and narrower than normal. It feels darker than other planes, clubby, more like a Town Car. The very nice businessman beside me once flew next to Michael Jackson, who amplified the claustrophobia of the experience by spending the entire flight with a blanket draped over his famous head.

The takeoff feels standard, not the vertiginous climb I was expecting. The captain comes on and warns the novices among us that after one minute and seventeen seconds, he will be turning off the "reheats." It will feel like we're suddenly losing speed and altitude, apparently, but it's nothing to worry about. Once we get out over the ocean, they can turn them back on again for the extra thrust. Reheats, I wonder? My neighbor tells me, "It's something incredibly dangerous, I think. Like they light the exhaust fumes. A bit like riding a huge firework."

Moore's law about information technology states that the transistors on integrated circuits will shrink to half their size every two years, until they are so small that they reach atomic widths. At that point, an entire paradigm shift will be needed to take computers further. It has been said that the demise of the Concorde represents that rarest of occurrences in civilization: a technological step backward. But the Concorde has always been more a triumph of consumption than of science. There's no great trick in getting people across the Atlantic in three hours. Burn twice as much fuel as a 747 and carry one quarter the payload. It is a beautifully controlled yet hideously wasteful bonfire. That it has continued to be in operation even this long is frankly amazing.

WE FLATTEN OUT for quite a while at a measly 6,000 feet and Mach .66 (about 470 mph). The crew is already up and walking around. At 12,500 feet we can unfasten our seat belts even though this is about one quarter of our target cruising altitude of 58,000 feet. I know all of this because there is no movie on the Concorde, nor are there any audio channels on the arm of my seat. What there is, and it makes for completely diverting and fascinating entertainment, is an LCD readout at the front of the cabin ticking off Mach speed and altitude.

We reach the speed of sound. I feel a little bit of g-force in the back of the teeth, but there is no discernible boom. Of course there wouldn't be, since it would be happening behind us. There is the definite tang in the air of burning fuel. Like smelling a recently used cigarette lighter.

At 42,000 feet and Mach 1.71 (1,110 mph), we are given some small canapés. Triple rounds of edible money: filet mignon topped with caviar, smoked salmon, foie gras and a gooseberry; followed by a salad of duck confit with still more foie gras and greens; and a cheese course. A glass of white wine, and three small chocolate truffles, flavored respectively with Earl Grey tea, passion fruit, and champagne. We are served on linen place mats and porcelain, but for post-9/11 safety's sake, the cutlery is all plastic, an empty concession since my napkin ring is a sharp-edged cuff of machine-cut stainless.

It's time to check out the promised phenomena. The window is warm, but the wall of the plane isn't. The curvature of the earth is extremely subtle, if visible at all. It's probably just the refraction of the fish-eye windows. As for the darkness of the stratosphere, it's a no-show. I ask the flight attendant. "Myths, all of it," she says. What about the red streak? She's heard tell but it, too, is erroneous. But, she says, the plane genuinely does expand with the heat, some eight to ten inches, in fact. This is most visible in the cockpit, where we are no longer allowed to go.

Something incredibly sweet happens at 56,000 feet and Mach 2. Something no one told me about: people come up to the front, easily twenty different individuals, to have their photographs taken beside the readout. They all smile for the camera, their faces like those of children, unashamedly delighted and amazed. The wonder of aviation revived, a full century into its innovation.

We land. Powerful, but again, no thrustier than usual. No Concorde-embossed gifts, alas, but who really needs one when you arrive in New York fully an hour before you even left London? I move through the airport like a man in love, dreamy and dancing and wanting to tell the world.

THAT CRAZY, CALLOW, buoyant feeling couldn't be further from the furtive embarrassment with which I skulk through the terminal at Newark Liberty International just a few short weeks later.

It was the Concorde's unsustainability, despite its two decades of operation, that ultimately rendered it the tangible cousin of utopian impracticalities like Smell-O-Vision and personal jetpacks. The foreseeable future of air travel is neither superfast nor super-exclusive. I have come to Newark to experience flying for the capitalist masses aboard the latest example of the new populism. Although, for something supposedly available to one and all, it is proving very difficult to find. I walk the concourse three times, looking fruitlessly for my carrier. After half an hour, I break down and ask a security guard, my voice a discreet mumble, where I might find the check-in counter for Hooters Air.

The ticket agent is handling a number of airlines. He only asks me where I'm going. When I respond with Myrtle Beach,

South Carolina, we both know why I'm there. Our transaction is encoded, like I'm visiting a whorehouse. I remind myself repeatedly that there is no reason to be embarrassed, paraphrasing perhaps the most un–Hooters Girl of them all, Eleanor Roosevelt: no one can humiliate me without my consent. Although it is not for lack of trying. At the metal detectors the security guard, an older Trinidadian woman, takes one look at my boarding pass and lets out a high, fluting "Hoot hoot!" before breaking into cackles of laughter.

Hooters Air was started in 2003 by the restaurant chain known for its chicken wings and hyper-mammalian waitresses. Every flight has three attendants who are dressed in traditional airline uniforms and trained in safety procedures, and two Hooters Girls, who aren't and aren't.

The aircraft arrives at the gate. White and orange with a blue racing stripe, the restaurant's owl logo graces the tail fin. The curious bird's eyes are bugged out in voyeuristic shock, forming the "OO" in the name. There is no rush among those of us waiting to photograph the plane through the windows. Numbering just eleven individuals, we are four more passengers than the seven who disembark. Behind them, the two Hooters Girls, one blond, one brunette, emerge dressed in body-covering track suits in sherbet-orange viscose. This is their more modest walking-around-the-airport attire. They look like Olympic athletes representing the tackiest country on earth, which I guess they kind of are.

They return in time to board before us and peel down to their uniforms of white tank tops, orange shorts, ribbed white athletic socks, and white leather sneakers. (They also wear nude-tan hose to even out skin tone and give their legs that just-off-the-beach sun-burnished glow, although it's actually closer to a barbecue-chicken-under-heat-lamps shade of orange.) Their hair is styled, their makeup prom-ready. Our pilot is a heavily Southern young man with strawberry blond hair and rosy cheeks. He looks confidence-destroyingly young but is thirty-seven and already in his second piloting job. Previously, he was employed at American International Airways, a cargo carrier. I had been expecting some bitter old drunk, drummed out of legitimate service, barred from the pilot's lounge. There is no ignominy in this posting. I ask if he ever gets teased by air traffic control when he flies in or out of airports. Occasionally, but they usually seem to be jokes about chicken wings.

I sit across the aisle from a couple from Staten Island, a friendly Vin Diesel type and his fiancée girlfriend. She has a house down in Myrtle Beach, right near her grandmother.

The blonde takes the microphone. "Good morning everybody. [It is 7:45 in the evening.] I'm Heather and this is Jennifer. We're your Hooters Girls. See you once we're airborne!" The flight attendants prepare the cabin for takeoff while Heather and Jennifer chatter together in the front seat, having no training, safety or otherwise, for this gig. They work at the Colonial Mall Hooters in Myrtle Beach. Heather sees the Staten Island girl's engagement ring, and swoops down to take her hand and exclaim with unselfconscious awe over the diamond. It's congenial and casual here, from the piece of green gum stuck to the back of my stowed and secured tray table staring at me at eye level, to the fact that the flight attendants and the Hooters Girls all have the same song stuck in their heads. They repeatedly sing the refrain "One More Ti-yime," and break up laughing.

Normally, once we had reached cruising altitude, the Hooters Girls would be taking charge to lead a trivia contest, with Hooters-related questions, such as how many sauces do they have for their wings? (Six: mild, medium, hot, Spicy Jack, Three Mile, and 911.) Or, how many Hooters are there in Myrtle Beach? (Four.) Sadly, the airline just inaugurated its service from Baltimore that very day, so every available piece of schwag—golf balls, caps, etc.—that might have served as our prizes was pressed into service for the mucky-mucks on that maiden voyage.

Instead, they announce that Hooters T-shirts are for sale. The Vin Diesel guy gets up to model one of them. "What's your name?" Heather asks him.

"Mitch."

She looks scandalized. "Bitch?" she asks.

"Mitch."

Working a flight is preferable to a shift in the restaurant. It's easier, for one thing, and they get $13.50 an hour. The wage for waiting tables is paltry: less than $3.00 an hour plus tips, although a Hooters Girl can make a tidy sum at certain times of the year, like Harley-Davidson Week, for example. Although she cannot be more than twenty, and is half dressed and pneu-matically constructed in precisely the way that ogling crowds of hairy bikers go for in a big way, Jennifer talks about serving these Hell's Angels with no trace of fear or trepidation. She even proudly but casually mentions that, with the exception of Hooters, most businesses in Myrtle Beach close down during Black Bike Week (not black bikes, but African American bikers).

"Why do you think that is?" I ask.

"They're rude," she replies, although I'm not sure if she means the bikers or the area merchants.

Jennifer is from West Virginia and attends Carolina Coastal College. She is curious about my notebook, but cannot read my scrawl. She takes my pen to write: "I love Hooters [smiley face]." Not to be outdone, Heather writes, "Roses are red / Violets are blue / the shorter the shorts / the better the view."

I have swallowed all the signifiers of their presentation, so it comes as a bit of a shock—and a good dose of medicine—when I ask them what they do when not waiting tables. Heather has been accepted into a nursing program. To bide her time over the summer before it starts, she's taking microbiology again, just to keep up on it. She passed it once already. Jennifer is in marine sciences, studying sharks and planning on doing graduate work in Australia.

"Wow, marine biology," I say.

"Uh-uh. Marine *sciences*," she corrects me. "Biology's just part of it."

I briefly wonder if they're having me on, trafficking in that old take-down-the-hair-remove-the-horn-rims, "Miss Jones, you're beautiful" fantasy. But I don't suspect grad school plans are a turn-on for most guys. Besides, the hair is already down and the glasses are nowhere in sight.

The three flight attendants are in the back of the plane, as they have been for most of the flight, kneeling on the seats and leaning over the back to talk and laugh with the other passengers. One guy stands in the aisle with a bottle of beer. It's all very *Coffee, Tea or Me,* a hearkening back to those cusp-of-the-sexual-revolution days when "stews" were good-time gals and flying was largely the province of men. The party in the rear stays that way until about seven minutes to the end, when one of the attendants finally comes up front. "Carole!" she calls to the back. *We're landing!* she mouths, as if to hide the fact from the rest of us, even though the plane has been pitched downward in a descending pattern for the last half hour. It pleases me to find out that it in no way affects the safety of a plane if it lands with a tray table down and seat not in the upright position. My can of seltzer and cup are still in front of me as we touch down in the stifling, Prell-thick air of a South Carolina evening.

Later that night, walking along the highway from the Burger King back to my motel, I hug the shoulder of the road, clutching my Double Whopper with Cheese to my chest, careful not to let the bag be ripped from my arms by the powerful wakes kicked up by the eighteen-wheelers and semis roaring by. The grassy verge along the driveway to my lodgings is damp with humidity, my T-shirt is soaked through from my three-minute walk. Passing through the automatic doors, I am greeted with a blast of air-conditioning as salutary as a blood transfusion. The vending machines by the reception desk—the motel's version of a restaurant—blaze with a stained-glass opulence. I feed a dollar into the slot and in turn I am graced with a frosty bottle of Gatorade the color of the Caribbean Sea.

IT'S STILL CAUSE for wonder, this being in one place on the globe in the morning and somewhere else entirely by evening. Even if it is only here, sitting on my motel bed watching CNN, with the curtains illuminated by the glow of the splash pool outside. It's still lit up, though it's already close to midnight. I guess they keep it turned on just because they can.

J.D.V., M.I.A.

They say New York is a Twenty-Four-Hour Town. I suppose that's true, if by Twenty-Four-Hour Town they mean you can probably get a plate of eggs somewhere or wander bleeding into an emergency room for suturing. But in the wee, small hours, it can be a very quiet affair. It is not the round-the-clock party it purports to be. That's why stories about staying up late in New York so often seem imbued with a gin-soaked wistfulness, even this one about an exuberant late-night scavenger hunt through the streets of lower Manhattan. Or maybe it's just the memory of it that makes me want to reach for the bottle.

This escapade is called Midnight Madness, named after an

apparently crummy 1980 movie about a scavenger hunt starring David Naughton of Dr Pepper commercial fame. A sporadically annual affair, it is the brainchild of Mat Laibowitz, a monomaniacally brilliant young electrical engineer who has seen the film dozens if not hundreds of times.

I am part of the White Team, an apt color for us, since in comparison to our thirty-odd, twentysomething opponents, we are snowy-locked geriatrics. Jaime, our team captain, reads the preliminary instructions for how the hunt will work: "Each clue will lead you to the location where the next clue is hidden, and so on. When you find one, call into HQ immediately. This starts a one-hour timer. If you haven't found the next clue after one hour, you can call again for a hint. *One hour!?!?* Oh my god . . ." His voice trails off with a what-have-we-gotten-ourselves-into weariness. Or perhaps I am projecting. Anything that calls itself Midnight Madness by definition means we won't be going home anytime soon. It is scarcely eight o'clock in the evening. It has been a good while since 12:00 a.m. held much attraction for me beyond being a perfectly lovely time to be ensconced in the comfort of my own home, sitting in my underpants, contentedly worrying about something.

Our playing field is the eastern half of downtown Manhattan, a vast area comprising Battery Park, Wall Street, Chinatown, the Lower East Side, the Bowery, Little Italy, and NoLiTa, a term used to describe the neighborhood to the north of Little Italy, a few city blocks positively metastatic with handbag stores. It will be an evening of more than seven hours' duration and two hard-won insights, the first of which is that I am not a facile puzzler. Scratch that: it goes deeper than that. I both suck and blow at puzzles, riddles, and games of all sorts. I am a reasonably intelligent guy, but when called upon to bring to bear strategic thinking, a competitive nature, and smarts all at the same time, I don't show myself to be just an idiot but the very worst kind: the voluble dolt who has no idea how stupid he is. Case in point, the first clue that kicks off the game:

THREE
     Y
     E
     B
     R
     O
     W
     S

Clearly this means that we are to hie ourselves immediately to Manhattan's nearest outdoor Frida Kahlo painting. Even though I have never seen anything in the city that might remotely fit this description, and a Frida Kahlo painting would more fittingly have "One Eyebrow" as its clue, I say it like only a moron wouldn't know this, as though the slip of paper actually had "Go to the Frida Kahlo painting!" written on it. My voice is almost exasperated at how much time we're wasting just standing there *discussing*. One of our team members—thankfully a mathematician who does this sort of thing for a living—steps in and points out that the shape of the clue, the way it is written, might indicate something. Could it be referring to a street corner? Also, the shared "E" probably suggests that rather than looking to the meaning of the words themselves, perhaps we should look to the letters. An anagram, maybe, of Bowery and Hester? It takes him as long to solve it as it took you to read the preceding four sentences. But he is kind in addition to being clever. "Or we could," he says, looking at me politely, "go looking for a Frida Kahlo painting . . ." He trails off. The very air itself is embarrassed to carry the sound of his diplomacy.

It's a tight fit for all the teams on the corner of Bowery and Hester. We jostle up against one another benignly, like apples in a bathtub. A young man spies the message slipped between the metal grates of a shuttered jewelry store and hurriedly whispers to his teammates. But once a clue is found, it's essentially impossible to keep it from the other teams. All forty of us pick up on it within a matter of seconds. "Free Mumia Jamal Zealots" it reads.

"To the Tombs!" I cry, ready to lead the charge to the jail connected to the courthouse. My teammates indulge me by walking down there. It's a short stroll and it buys them some time away from the eyes of the other teams to come up with the true solution. They are very gentle with me as they try to get me to see beyond the obvious and look at things a little more obliquely, the meaning behind the meaning. That's the difference, say, between overt directions and a puzzle. "Yes, yes," I say, waving them off, picking up the pace. "We'd better get to the jail before the others."

They flash one another concerned looks, like the March sisters in *Little Women,* and I am Beth, the youngest, chattering brightly at Christmas about the piano recital I shall give that spring when it is clear to everyone else that I will surely be dead before they even run out of eggnog. I am a goner as far as being of any use in concerned, and still they sweetly make me feel as if I had some part in figuring out that it is the phrase's initials—F, M, J, Z and the subways they represent—that lead us to the Delancey Street subway station, the only hub of those four trains.

A TASK HAS to be just challenging enough to be engaging. A complicated model of Chartres cathedral might be rigorous and fun to try and put together, but not if the instructions suddenly switch over into Norwegian without warning. I am finding all this far too difficult, and batting zero is starting to wear me down. By 11:30, I am the walking illustration of Why Johnny Can't Read: I am frustrated and angry and no longer interested in even trying. I am the physical, as well as the intellectual, deadweight of the White Team, sitting on the subway stairs as the rest of them find and solve the clue. I am the sullen fourteen-year-old child none of my teammates knew they had or wanted. I dawdle behind as we climb the steps back above ground and over to a disused pissoir on the traffic median of a Lower East Side boulevard.

I shine my flashlight through the barred window of the small pavilion. The beam glances off the tiled, graffitied walls and old urinals, coming to rest on the floor where I see two photographs of the Artist Formerly Known As and the Queen of England. (How did the puzzlemaster even get in there, I wonder? The doors to the toilet are bricked shut.) The mere fact of finally getting a clue right shoots through me like an ampoule of adrenaline. I am suddenly energized and awake as we race over to the intersection of Prince and Elizabeth. But my good mood burns off like morning fog as we stand around for an hour near a restaurant called Peasant. (*Darling, have you been? Their gruel? Simply too delicious. We ate our entire meal languishing in their adorable little debtor's prison in the basement, and then the children died of rickets! Divine!*)

None of the teams has any idea. The most avid puzzlers among us are stumped. We walk up and down the sidewalk, pressing our faces through the iron bars of the fence of the tombstone manufacturer, scanning for the umpteenth time the wheat-pasted broadside of Jerry Garcia stuck to the mailbox. Sleepiness and a congenital simplemindedness have me using my already flimsy powers of deduction on analyzing garbage. I study a drippy soda can for messages like it was the Rosetta stone.

Eventually, a collective "uncle" is declared, and someone calls in to Midnight Madness HQ on behalf of all of us. "Look at your feet," we are told, and there, suspended from a sidewalk grating by colored tabs, are envelopes hanging down into the sewer. We fish them out and find locker keys and a clue that leads us to our next location: the South Ferry terminal.

It is now well after 2:00 a.m. as we scramble for cabs to take us to the bottom of the island. *This taxi is going the wrong way,* I think, as block by block my apartment becomes ever more distant. Looking out the windows to my left and right, I see that we are a fleet ten vehicles strong, almost the only cars on the road right now. For all my innate incapacity to actually enjoy myself, I am at least able to grasp just how impressive this entire enterprise is. It's beautifully organized and even more beautiful in its execution. Some of the clues are complete works of art. The one waiting for us in the Delancey Street subway station was a perfect replica of one of those official "change in service" notices routinely posted by the transit authority. We walked by it at least ten times. I also have to give it to Mat, the game master who put this together: spending a Saturday night in New York engaged in an actual activity that doesn't involve the usual $30 restaurant expenditure is a very nice change. There's something inherently cool about Midnight Madness, even though this is among the geekiest things I've ever done.

Mat—whose almost parodic nerdiness is only amplified by the fact that he is as lovely as Montgomery Clift and seems to have no idea—fully agrees: "Geek, when used correctly, is usually a compliment. It means eccentric, skilled, quirky, unique." Mat is constantly building something. For as long as he can remember, he has taken apart everything he has ever owned and reassembled it into something else. The intricate problems associated with coordinating Midnight Madness make him happy. It's no great revelation that he and I might have different ideas of what constitutes a good time, but the intrinsically *Rashōmon* quality of almost all shared experience never fails to surprise me. When Jaime complains at one point of sore feet and says how there isn't a chance in hell he would ever do this again, I feel a deep and throbbing love for him. But when he gets his second wind not twenty minutes later, the keen knife blade of betrayal slices through me and I hate no one on this earth as much as horrible, turncoat Jaime. People are rarely in sync. I know what my favorite moment of the night is. I ask Mat to tell me his.

"Battery Park," he says. "I got to see everyone at that time and walk around. That to me was really nice."

He is not entirely wrong. It was an enormous relief to get out of the bus-station-bright fluorescence of the deserted ferry terminal, and a bonus that the park was just a short walk across the street into the velvet darkness of the trees with the lapping of the Hudson River nearby. We all gathered at the World War II memorial. It's a starkly beautiful plaza right by the water with about a dozen huge concrete slabs, easily twenty feet square, engraved with the names of the dead. Players shone their flashlights over the tablets like archaeologists in the Valley of the Kings. The clues—dredged up from the opaque depths of the river, kept dry in ziplock bags, their presence in the black water indicated by those fluorescent Glow Sticks teenagers wave at rock concerts—were complex acrostics with letter and number combinations corresponding to the names and dates on the monuments. This was the final clue of the evening, which would lead us to the secret location of the Midnight Madness wrap party.

It was probably great fun for Mat to emerge from the command center and see the fruits of his labor after a long night of fielding calls. I might even agree with him had it been during the day. But it was close to four in the morning at that point. Rats were audibly, fearlessly scurrying through the bushes nearby, and mosquitoes—their thoraxes no doubt full to bursting with West Nile virus—buzzed incessantly about our ears. That was also when Jaime ran into a friend of his. This friend was not part of our game. He was there for other reasons. Gentle reader, I will let you in on something: if you are a gay man strolling of a summer's night through a dark New York City park sometime after 3:30 a.m., there is a reason for it and that reason is not so you will run into someone you know. In fact, the last person you want to run into is someone you know. Let me amend that: the second-to-last person you want to run into is someone you know. The truly *very* last person you want to run into is someone you know accompanied by dozens of jolly amateur sleuths.

With flashlights.

JAIME'S FRIEND BEATS a hasty retreat back into the darker regions of the park where he can continue to follow his bliss. The time has come for me to follow my own, as well. The bliss of the quitter, the killjoy, the pill.

I joined in at Jaime's urging because, like most people, I like to think of myself as being spontaneous, ready for anything, fun. This is the evening's second hard-won insight: I am neither spontaneous nor ready for anything. I suspect that others would probably regard this news as about as momentous and surprising as when I decided to come out (which was about as momentous and surprising as if I had bravely announced to everyone that I had dark hair and opposable thumbs). I am no fun at all. In fact, I am anti-fun. Not as in anti-violence, but as in anti-matter. I am not so much against fun—although I suppose I kind of am—as I am the direct opposite of fun. I suck the fun out of a room. Or perhaps I'm just a different kind of fun; the kind that leaves one bereft of hope; the kind of fun that ends in tears.

BIDDING MY FRIENDS good night, I emerge from the park and hail a cab. It is now that time of night where at the end of *La Dolce vita* Marcello Mastroianni and his friends make their bleary trek through the woods down to the seashore. There is nothing more to drink and no one left to corrupt or use up. When I first moved here at the age of seventeen, I thought there would be lots of nights like this, staying out until all hours and crawling home with the proverbial milkman (I've never seen an actual milkman in my life). And while I spend my days paddling through a stew of regrets, a youth not spent shouting over the sound system in some after-hours venue isn't one of them. Besides, I have seen my share of New York sunrises. During an eight-year stretch of insomnia I saw almost all of them, pottering around the apartment until it was time to shower and go to work.

Dawn is picking out and lightening the cornices of façades as we hurtle up through a deserted Wall Street. Settling into the backseat, I am reminded of that Wislawa Szymborska poem that used to be posted in subway cars. Something about how no one feels fine at 4:00 a.m. If the ants feel fine at 4:00 a.m., then hooray for the ants. Hooray for me, too. I am on my way home to bed, if not exactly sleep, the preferred nocturnal activity of most people in this great, big, dirty burg. This is my favorite moment of the night.

PRIVATES ON PARADE

The building at the corner of Forty-sixth Street and Broadway that houses the Howard Johnson's is also the home of the billboard for the revival of the musical *Chicago*. If you were to peel it back, you might discover a forgotten window, and hanging in it, a sign touting the long defunct Whirly Girly Revue. Who can say what the original colors were? By the time I became aware of it, around 1982, it had already been bleached by more than twenty years' worth of Times Square sunlight, its type faded to pale Crest-blue against a yellowing french-vanilla background. The Whirly Girly was probably a 1950s establishment, from the looks and lexicon of the sign. The lettering, block printing with vaguely exaggerated dimensions—the arms of the *y*s arcing like wishbones—tried to mimic some of the verve and curve of the good times promised inside. It's probably still there. There would have been little reason for its removal. Much easier to just leave it, covered over with the images of Bob Fosse's barely clad, hard-boiled Prohibition-era cutie-pies. It's like a geological record of peek-aboo, the layers moving you back and forth through time with the ease of a trombone slide.

Nostalgia has always been a bit of a bunko scam. Authentic charms of its signage notwithstanding, it's worth remembering that those must have been some pretty grim circumstances for the young ladies of the Whirly Girly. Unless it's your own heyday as a peepshow dancer you're fondly recalling, it's dangerous to drag a sepia-dipped brush over the sleaze of yesteryear. By early November of 2001, there is no need to look to the past for our daily dose of tawdry. While the rest of the country has wrapped itself in the flag and emerged newly patriotic and bellicose, New York scarcely two months after September 11 has tempered the jingoism by rising like a drunken, horny phoenix from its ashes. The city is electric with the renewed crackle of filth. Chalk it up to that old market-theory chestnut about the rising hemline in the plummeting economy, or that people simply don't want to spend their nights alone. The media have coined a term for the transitory love-in-wartime clutches they claim are happening everywhere: Terror Sex.

While I have balanced the many weeks that I spent crying in front of the news with embracing the obliviating powers of alcohol, I've yet to dip my spoon into any of that Thanatosscented carnality. So I have come up to Forty-second Street to witness the new Weimar firsthand. Secondhand, actually, as I will only be a passive audience member of *Puppetry of the Penis.*

The proscenium of the John Houseman Theater has been decorated like a Greek temple with PENIS TEMPUS inscribed on the pediment. The audience is made up of mixed couples and groups of women. I spy one male duo. I am the only single man. I make very conspicious use of my notebook. No one cares anyway. They have been buying beer and wine in the lobby and have been encouraged to bring their drinks into the theater with them. One woman comes in carrying a pizza box and a stack of napkins and the ushers make no move to stop her. Her friends, a gaggle of girls out for a night on the town, wave her over. The pizza is for later, I suppose, because for now the ladies are sucking lewdly on heart-shaped lollipops. Even though the temple onstage has a Latin designation, it feels quite Greek in here. I mean Greek in that binge-drinky, Dalíesque-arcs-of-airborne-vomit, ripe-with-the-incipient-danger-of-date-rape, college-fraternity sense of the word, as opposed to the Aegean birthplace of democracy.

The house fades to black and the man of the young couple beside me puts his arm protectively around his date. "Pray silence for the keeper of the art. Priapus!" says a recorded voice as a roly-poly young man in a short toga and paper laurel wreath takes the stage.

"In Rome, they call me Dionysus. In India, Shiva. In Wales, Tom Jones." I am too busy writing *Rome was Bacchus, no?* in my notebook to truly register the moment, but the evening's zenith of wit has just come and gone. Priapus introduces the two stars and creators of the show, Simon Morley and David Friend. The two Australians come out in velvet capes, their bare ankles disappearing into puffy white sneakers, not unlike Heather and Jennifer, my Hooters Girls. Doffing their garments, they stand naked before us, to the loud hoots and hollers and shocked chuckles of the audience. The young man beside me takes his arm from his girlfriend's shoulders and folds his hands in his lap.

Neither Morley nor Friend has a particularly nice body. Maybe if it was more of a treat to see them naked, I might feel less embarrassed, able to get into the proceedings more. But then I remember the time I accompanied the writer Dan Savage to the Gaiety Male Burlesque on Forty-sixth Street, not far from the storied Whirly Girly.

Dan was doing research on the seven deadly sins, and I went along to watch the strippers. Even there, the onstage antics of the naked men, some of them startlingly handsome, were curiously unerotic. That hypothetical question that I kept on asking myself while watching them shoot *Sesión Privada*—would I be more aroused if these were guys?—was answered in pretty short order at the Gaiety. The drill was the same with each dancer: he came out wearing very little, danced quite badly—the strippers were largely, easily identifiably straight—and then went offstage while the very well-behaved audience waited. In a perfect world, he was supposed to come back onstage starkers and erect. In an evening of twelve or so dancers, Dan and I only saw one instance of tumescence. The boner got some polite clapping, like the entrance applause that greets an ingenue who has received very good advance notices:

("Why, here comes Alice now."

"Hello, Pat . . ." she says, swanning onto the stage in tennis whites. She pauses before delivering the rest of her line. Facing the audience, she makes a slight bow of grateful recognition of her effect upon them. "It was so awfully swell of you to invite me.")

AT *PUPPETRY,* IT becomes immediately clear that the men's bodies are nothing more than the utilitarian walls of flesh from which their units depend. The show is strictly about their genital origami, as they call it. Their soft bellies and flat dimpled asses fade from view, not for the least reason because Priapus—O multitasking deity slash unpaid intern!—is filming all of it on video in tight, tight close-up, which is then projected in huge magnification against the upstage wall. This is the world's least appetizing cooking show. Today, chicken gizzards!

They begin with the Wind-up, stretching and turning their dicks like auto cranks while calliope music plays. Priapus was the wrong muse to invoke. Plastic Man would have been more apt, because the evening requires some very un-priapic slackened flesh. These guys aren't unnaturally well endowed so much as pulled. There will be future hell to pay for both of them, urologically and aesthetically.

"None of these hurt at all, so we don't want you to feel sorry for us," says one of them. But I can't help it. I do feel sorry for them. Sorrier still for their mothers, and sorriest of all for myself.

They call their tricks "installations," and from the very first one, the Woman, where Morley tucks his leading man between his legs, the audience is beside itself with laughter. The banter would have to be smartened up tenfold to qualify as idiotic. It's all just a series of card tricks. "Here's another, the Wristwatch," he announces as a penis is wrapped around a forearm. "Who wants a hamburger?" (I don't.)

The installations are trotted out one after another with all the dramatic flair of a shopping list. I keep on waiting for some commentary, a story, anything resembling a point, so to speak. Friend does at least provide us with a bit of *Puppetry* lore. "Quite a lot of our installations were developed in a pub environment," he says. *Say, kids, why don't we take our drunken, latent homoerotic urges and turn them into a socko show?*

I sit through the Loch Ness Monster and the Roller Skate but leave just as they begin introducing props with the Squirrel, a glans poking through a knothole in a piece of bark. Perhaps my impression of the overall piece is woefully misinformed by my partial viewing, but failing a wholesale shift to Strindberg in the final thirty minutes, I don't think so.

"You're not going, are you?" asks a member of the house staff in the lobby, her voice as astonished as if I had risen from the operating table mid-appendectomy. But I have to leave. *Penis Tempus* just didn't *fugit* fast enough.

———

THERE IS MUCH in our culture to affront the eye of the fervent terrorist postulant, things out there that do us no favors, to be sure. If, for example, it came to light that the dangerously thin, affectless, value-deficient, higher aspiration–free, amateur-porn *auteuse* Paris Hilton was actually a covert agent from some secret Taliban madrassa whose mission was to portray the ultimate capitalist-whore puppet of a doomed society with nothing more on its mind than servitude to Mammon and celebrity at any cost, I wouldn't be a bit surprised. But unless Al Qaeda has some extra-special religious proscription against the idiotic and sophomoric, I'd be hard-pressed to count *Puppetry of the Penis* among those transgressive things that make us glorious and free. As a work of degenerate art, it is neither. It's harmless. The embarrassment I feel as I exit the John Houseman is not in having a penis of my own. It is in having retinas. And this might sound like a strange thing to say about a spectacle wherein two men spend more than an hour onstage stark naked but for shoes pulling the old dog-and-dice every which way for our delectation, but it lacked good old-fashioned showmanship. I've seen children's magic shows with more engaging narrative flow, let alone more convincing balloon animals. I thought rude sideshow entertainments like this vanished long ago due to such civilizing influences as universal inoculation and the Tennessee Valley Authority.

The rest of the audience adores it, though. After all, Joseph Pujol, the nineteenth-century star of the Moulin Rouge, has a street named after him in Paris. He delighted common folk and crowned heads alike with demonstrations of his *péto-*

manie, or "fartistry," doing birdcalls and even blowing out the footlights onstage from quite a distance, using nothing more than his remarkable flatulent powers, so what do I know?

Maybe this is just what folks need right now, I think, trying to be charitable. The final tally of the dead changes every day and the subterranean fires at Ground Zero only recently stopped burning. There is still the ever-present question of further attack hanging over our heads. And talk about reports of the death of irony being premature, the tenure of Mayor Rudolph Giuliani—the martinet who improved the city for the few by abridging the rights of the many and criminalizing poverty—had the greatest final act in history, as he underwent his surreal transformation into a beloved hero, even, albeit briefly, to the liberal public-television totebag–oisie who roundly loathed him through two terms. It had been an aggressively rough two months in the city at that point.

I WALK THROUGH the heart of Times Square to the subway. I hadn't been up there since the morning of September 12, when I stood on line outside the *New York Times* building on Forty-third Street to buy the newspaper; they couldn't be found for love or money elsewhere in the city. About 150 of us waited for the papers to be delivered from the printing plant.

The trucks were taking longer than expected and I had promised friends that I would buy papers for them, too. I knew they would be worried about me if I was late so I turned to the woman behind me and asked if I could pay her a dollar to use her cell phone.

She thought about it for a second. "Hmmmm . . . No. I don't want to use up my minutes."

Not her batteries, that she would need in good working order to call for help, god forbid, were she trapped underneath some fallen rubble, but her minutes. A purchasable commodity that I was in fact offering to purchase. Oddly enough, I found this display of cuntiness not twenty-four hours after tragedy bracingly restorative. We were still intact after all.

I was also in Times Square on the first night of Desert Storm, oddly enough. Emerging from a movie late at night, I stood in the snow with half a dozen others watching the lights of the news zipper telling us that war had been declared. *This is just like that photograph of the sailor kissing the nurse,* I thought, with a too-healthy dose of self-mythologizing grandiosity, ignoring for the moment that that was a picture on the day the war ended, and in this instance the casualties were about to begin piling up.

IN THE WEEKS following September 11, when people were questioning whether they should stay in town, my friend Jenny wondered aloud at supper one evening, "Do you think we're like those photographs of happy Berliners walking along the boulevards in 1938, completely blind to what's about to happen?" I'm not sure how happy or oblivious Berliners really were even in 1938, but I know what she means. It has been difficult to know how to behave, what to do. Another friend had to be seriously talked down from hightailing it to the Maine woods. There was a photo of a young woman in the

Times a few days earlier. She said something to the effect that she did not, in point of fact, find it pleasant to be living in epic times. I quite agree.

THE NOVEMBER AIR is cloudy with a frozen mist that makes halos around the lights of Forty-second Street, giving the place an old-timey sodium glow. I am reminded of something newspaperman and playwright Ben Hecht wrote in 1941 about Times Square. He wondered if, in half a century, the things he beheld then and there might seem "part of a scene so quaint and human as will bring tears to the eyes of some old print connoisseur in the year 1991. The electromania of Broadway, these neon and electric signs, the hemorrhage of lights, how full of a vanished individualism they will seem. What of the newspaper headlines? Will they also seem like valentines? Here is a more difficult metamorphosis to imagine. Hitler on a valentine!" Hecht is prescient. I've never seen an image of der Führer with the words "Be mine," but *The Producers,* the Yiddish-inflected Mel Brooks musical, has a full-on Busby Berkeley Hitler number and is still running to packed houses.

I ride back downtown, coming aboveground at Union Square. The city's biggest spontaneous memorial sprang up here mere hours after the attacks. By now, the place where crowds gathered to stand in silence has devolved over the weeks into a skeleton crew of die-hard youngsters engaged in drumming circles, Ultimate Frisbee games, and the free exchange of genital warts. I pass by a small group of them, playing guitar and still sitting on the grass even though it's promising to be a cold night. Littered around them are the wax plugs of candle ends, empty votive cups scattered here and there on the ground, and stray leaflets of the missing, sodden with rain, baked by the sun, now illegible and curling like dying leaves. Surrounded by all these multicolored bits and pieces, these kids could be the last stragglers at a fantastic party. Maybe there is some solace to be derived in that: bacchanal or funeral, after enough time, the detritus looks the same.

BEACH BUMMER

The scene is by now part of our collective unconscious: the earth being churned from underneath, a snaking runnel suddenly rupturing forth like a keloid scar. The burrowing stops abruptly and up from the ground pops Bugs Bunny, jubilant, his holiday props of pail and shovel at the ready. "Miami Beach!" he declaims. "Yippee! Hooray! Yahoo-y!" and off he runs, racing across the burning sand to the water. But Bugs has indeed taken that left turn at Albuquerque and is nowhere near Miami Beach. Hours later, we find him trudging half dead across a desert, searching in vain for an ocean.

Some might interpret this as a parable about the miragelike futility of dreams. Still others might choose to see it as nothing more than the wascally wabbit's chance to indulge in his penchant for drag in order to outsmart that hot-tempered bedouin he will meet later on in the cartoon. Personally, the message I take away is that, in contrasting it favorably with the punishing emptiness of the vast, arid Sahara, what Bugs Bunny and his creators don't know about Miami Beach is a whole lot.

It is not the fault of South Beach that I am a joy-obliterating erotophobe. That it comprises some of my deepest aversions (heat, direct sunlight, and a pervasive sense of fun) while lacking many of my most cherished requirements in a destination (occasional rain, the generally suppressive influence of the superego, and a melancholic populace prone to making mono-chrome woodcuts of hollow-eyed women sitting disconsolate in shabby rooms with their meager suppers on tin plates before them) is nobody's problem but my own. And it's a problem that I will have to keep to myself this weekend as I work the pool at one of Miami's hiply refurbished art deco hotels—the Hiawatha, let's call it.

In the old days of Miami, when there was still a vital demographic that I might have charmed with my smattering of Yiddish, my pool duties would probably have involved setting up deck chairs and opening striped umbrellas, with perhaps the odd slather of cocoa butter across the occasional expanse of freckled dowager's back. But those are the klezmer strains of a largely disappeared world. The old widows have either died off or sit wheelchair-bound in nursing homes. The fever dream that is the new South Beach is all sleek, adamantine hedonism. I will be at the beck and call of a clientele glossy with privilege: glamorous people of low degree with tight clothing and loose morals.

I can already see myself approaching a poolside cabana, a large cream-colored canvas tent providing a conspicuous privacy. Pushing aside the flap, I deliver drinks to a music impresario and his two friends. On a chaise nearby, the mogul's girlfriend lies, a living Helmut Newton photograph in nothing but Manolos and panties, her eyes rolled up into the back of her head, the glossed lips of her somnolent mouth parted. Beside her a small black-lacquered table frosted with a conical pile of cocaine, wispy traces of it wicking off in the slight breeze.

"Here, get rid of this," says one of the minions, a still-warm Glock clattering onto my tray.

"Certainly, sir," I reply as I back out, my heart beating against the three crisp hundred-dollar bills he has folded and slipped into my shirt pocket.

I'd turn down an invitation to Nero's orgy as a guest, but the judgmental voyeur in me would jump at the chance to man the coat check at same.

THE NIGHT BEFORE I start work, I take a walk along the beach to get the lay of the land. The deco palaces of Collins Avenue are welcoming young revelers to their respective pool and bar scenes, their outdoor sound systems starting their nightly battle. The music and laughter signal the official shift from late afternoon to early evening. The sky is a bruise of mauve and pink. A huge silver moon hangs out over the water which, even at dusk, is still a startling blue-green. Washed up everywhere on the sand are crescent-shaped jellyfish; transparent gyoza edged in bright blue and crimson. Turning away from the ocean I face the hotels once more, a floodlit chorus line of wedding cakes packed so close together that one could scarcely slip a knife blade between them. A future bride opens the gifts at her shower, occasioning a regular chorus of "whoo-hoo" from her drunk friends. In their matching magenta feather boas, they are easy to spot. I can still make them out in the gathering darkness.

"THE AMBASSADOR CAN own the pool. You can really set the tone of the place," says Vivienne, the Hiawatha's front-office manager, during my training session. Pool Ambassador is a little-known diplomatic posting whose primary task is making sure that the people coming down the steps from the hotel or up from the beach are actual paying guests. I am to check their names against a list. I am a doorman without a door. And that is all, it seems. The Hiawatha pool is staffed by a veritable pantheon of minor non-deities, each of us with an individual and specialized role. There are two young women who keep the chaises covered with fresh towels and clear away the wet ones, two bartenders, one waiter, and two Ambassadors: myself and Sammy, a recent Miami transplant from New York also starting his stint poolside that very day.

Sammy and I are sitting at a long walnut table in the Hiawatha's conference room, a glass-walled cube off the lobby, rendered private with curtains of sheer white fabric. Our joint training session is a high-powered affair. The top three members of the hotel's staff, including the general manager and head of housekeeping, have gathered to instruct just the two of us.

"You'll have your eye out for things," Vivienne continues, putting the best face on the situation. "Say you overhear that it's a guest's birthday. You could tell one of the front-office staff, and we could arrange for a cake to be delivered to their room. We'd like to be that kind of hotel."

We are reminded to smile. We must never let a problem show in front of a guest. Establish eye contact and use a guest's name if possible. Above all, we are told, we are to learn the subtle distinction between being friendly but not friends. "I would draw the line at applying the sunscreen," says Vivienne.

I feel underutilized and I haven't even begun, but if it's benevolent omniscience they want, then I will be the self-effacing, eagle-eyed mole of their dreams, pervasive and invisible as a gas leak. Nothing will escape my purview. Unsolicited birthday cakes arriving at hotel room doors? Kid stuff. I will save marriages by discreetly whispering into a husband's ear that perhaps he might like to wish his wife a happy anniversary while I slip a thoughtfully purchased necklace of black freshwater pearls into his hand, before rushing up to the helipad on the hotel roof (note to self: verify existence of helipad) to meet the human liver packed on ice that I have surreptitiously arranged for the little girl languishing on her poolside gurney, waiting in vain for a donor. *What ever would we do without you, Pool Ambassador?*

The training continues. We should greet any guest within three feet, but need only acknowledge one within ten with a nod or a smile. I'm on it, already planning how to measure the distance using the ancient art of triangulation, my body and the shadow it casts a primitive sundial. We are to be the first to begin the conversation, and should have the last word, as well. Say no more. But why content myself with the suggested "Have a nice afternoon," when I can make a guest's day by uttering the far more meaningful—and in the moment that I say it, absolutely true—"I love you" to their departing form? I am vibrating with excitement to get out there and prove just how mewlingly subservient I can be. The more tortuous the etiquette instruction in the training session, the more hopped up I get. Maybe it was all the years I spent answering other people's phones and doing their bidding, or maybe it's just low self-esteem, but it turns out that I'm very good at the hyper-polite, obsequious bow and scrape. In the right situation, highly formalized, high-suction ass-kissing not only comes all too naturally to me, it makes me breathless with a feeling of penitential power.

THE POOL IS a hidden-edge rectangle surrounded by brushed-aluminum deck chairs. It sits at the end of the Hiawatha's long green lawn, framed by palms. I introduce myself to my co-workers and take up my position by the gate leading out to the beach. Even though we were told not to talk to one another for extended periods of time—it makes the guests uncomfortable if they feel like they're interrupting a conversation—Sammy immediately comes over to my side of the pool and stands chatting for half an hour. He has worked at the Hiawatha in other jobs. Sotto voce, he tells me to be careful, cocking an eyebrow over to Luiz, one of the bartenders. "He's a snake."

Our shift is from 10:00 a.m. to 6:00 p.m. By 10:15, the pool area is filling up with the guests who don't seem remotely connected with the criminal element, alas. A gorgeous young couple arrive with their baby and nanny, a group of middle-aged ladies from Los Angeles in town shooting a commercial, and a trio made up of two women and a straight man with a gay body. Limbs are greased, magazines are thumbed through, someone tempts the collapse of the space-time continuum by reading *The South Beach Diet* in South Beach. Sleepy conversation is droned back and forth as they tan.

My cheeks already ache from the Mona Lisa smile I have on my face, ready to ratchet it up into a full-fledged toothy grin for anyone who so much as glances in my general direction. A man in a black Speedo says something to me. I walk over eagerly, his wish my command, but as I get closer I see his eyes lack focus, like a sleepwalker, and I only spot his cell phone headset once I am within three feet of him, at which distance I am required by the protocols of my Ambassadorship to greet him, which I do, heartily.

"Uh, hi," he responds, interrupted.

"Need anything?" I ask.

He's okay for the moment. I resume my position on the travertine walkway, feet together, arms crossed over my clipboard. My posture is ramrod straight. I look like one of the Coldstream guards in front of Buckingham Palace but all I am really trying to do is stay in the very narrow band of shade cast by a palm tree. The fronds clatter in the breeze overhead like venetian blinds.

The morning crawls by, my dreams of indispensability deferred and I the whitest raisin in the sun. Radu, the pool's waiter, a large pink-and-white wall of a man who resembles an affable overgrown baby, takes orders and delivers drinks, having lots of conversations. I hate Radu.

We are allowed a thirty-minute break for lunch. My co-Ambassador, Sammy, takes an hour and returns without a word of apology. I run to the Burger King on the corner. I wonder what it is about my uniform—an outfit consisting of a white T-shirt with navy banding at the cuffs, a blue-and-white grosgrain belt, white shorts, and white sneakers—that immediately marks me as wearing one. In college, I briefly favored pajama tops as shirts, until one of my professors leaned over one day and confidentially told me, "You know, no one would know if it wasn't for the buttons." She was right. They were the size of Mentos. With my Hiawatha uniform, I think it's a combination of the fact that if you're all in white on Collins Avenue, that means you're in service, coupled with my clothes' fastidious cleanliness but rather casual approximation of proper fit. I'd hoped to be wearing something a little tighter and sexier. My present loose attire only accentuates my unmistakable forty years of wear and tear, the love handles, and male pattern baldness. I project the wide-assed sexlessness of a dad. In other words, I am invisible in South Beach. Exactly what a uniform is designed to do.

It is blessedly air-conditioned in the Burger King and lovely chamber music plays. I wolf down my chicken sandwich and head back to the hotel. I pass by some Hiawatha guests I had greeted at the pool not minutes before. More decently attired in street clothes, they look straight at me without recognition.

By late afternoon the pool is—oh sweet, merciful God!—cast in shade. I won't die of heat stroke but the inertia might kill me. Ambassador duties be damned, I make the unilateral decision to help take the foam cushions from the chaises and stack them in a storeroom for the night. Just moving around fulfilling this simplest of tasks brightens my mood immeasurably. It makes the last half hour of my shift pass in a way it hasn't all day long.

My first day is almost over. The morning crowd has left the pool. Three blond Southern women come down and take seats at the bar. They are boisterous, cracking jokes with the staff. One of the women is on a cell phone and motions me over and makes a writing gesture. I proffer my pen and clipboard, and she scribbles down a phone number and finishes up her call. I tear off the slip of paper and hand it to her. "Thank you, darlin', I've been drinking since noon," she says, letting me in on her not terribly well-kept secret. She holds up the phone number for her cronies. "Lookit what I did to this handsome man's paper!" She grabs both of my hands in both of hers and spins me around with a high-pitched laughing "Wheeeew!" A brief Virginia reel to end my day. Her friends watch her with mild amusement. This is clearly not her first dance of the day with a strange man.

"That is some L.P.," one of them says to me. "Loud pussy."

AT NO TIME is the strangeness of this charade starker than in the mornings. I am staying two hotels over from the Hiawatha. My room is the most gorgeously appointed surgery on earth: white floor, white walls, white bed, white desk, white phalaenopsis orchid. As I wait for my breakfast in my white terrycloth robe, I think, *I hope room service arrives on time so I'm not late for my fake job.*

The twenty-second commute leaves me with some time to kill so I take a walk farther along Collins Avenue. The main strip of beautifully refurbished hotels gradually gives way to smaller, two-story guesthouses, seedy with disrepair, their pastel-colored plaster bubbling, all sweet green icing flowing down into the tiny front yards with their scrubby, dusty palms. It's a small pocket of the seventies here, before the district was landmarked, when it was still just a boneyard for abandoned grandmothers. Loose windowpanes rattle in rusty casements, a rainbow flag hangs tattered and proud over an iron balcony, lending the place the battle-scarred dignity of a gay Alamo.

It is sunbaked and sad, a redundancy in my photophobic universe. Two blocks farther on I come upon the near future of this dilapidation: the low-lying luxury of Ocean Drive. The sidewalk is crowded with tables and umbrellas as vacationers tuck into $15 plates of eggs in one hundred percent humidity. In front of the Gianni Versace mansion a man takes a picture of a woman. While he is focusing, she jokingly puts her index finger to her forehead and shoots. *Kapow.* "Hold that!" he instructs her, laughing.

FROM MY NOTES, written in the margins of the guest list: "Day 2: I have had five brief interactions, put up two umbrellas, ordered two drinks (which I did not deliver). A bright, moss green salamander on the trunk of a palm tree. I point it out to some of the kids. I'm going to help with towels today, I think. Might get to do some food and beverage stuff, too. Hope so."

I have written the above paragraph, or something like it, countless times before; some version of this minutely dissected narrative of self-consciousness whenever I begin a job. Even this three-day imposture—where they cannot fire me because they never really hired me—has me nervously listing my accrual of small tasks. I am desperate to look busy and efficient, and trying to establish a beachhead of comfort.

The heat and the back and forth of a small plane pulling its banner up and down the beach, CENTRO ESPANOL 100 GoGo GIRLS DESNUDAS, are hypnotic. A confrontation at the beach gate of the hotel directly next door jolts me from my torpor. An older couple is being ejected. He has gray-blond hair in tight curls and looks not unlike Lamb Chop, the ventriloquist's puppet. A medallion glints on his bronzed chest. She is outfitted in the height of Saint-Tropez fashion, circa 1978—white bikini, a gold chain around her waist, a bright gold clip in her tousled blond hair, gold high-heeled cork wedgies. They are both cancerously tan and surprisingly buff, given that neither of them has seen seventy in a number of years. They could be escapees from a Jews of the Diaspora exhibit crafted out of beef jerky.

"You're a nasty motherfucker, you know that?" the man says, presumably to next door's Pool Ambassador. He continues to hurl invective until they totter off. I am so bored I think wistfully, *I wish someone was ripping* me *a new asshole*.

At 1:30, an enormous black cloud the size of the entire neighborhood passes overhead, and about twenty-seven drops fall from the sky. I pray that it will storm and cool things down. Actually, my prayers go deeper and more apocalyptic than that. I pray that refrigerator-sized hailstones will rain down and obliterate all of us. Too bad for me, by 1:42 the cloud has blown over.

THERE WILL BE a sunset wedding on Sunday evening on the roof (no helipad). A number of our guys are there setting up, leaving the pool serviced by a skeleton crew. An elderly Chinese woman is sitting in the sun, her hands folded over the railing of her steadily heating metal walker. She looks stoic but dehydrated so I walk over and take her order. This *infuriates* Sammy, who feels that if we are short-staffed it is due to bad management. I should let the guests sit and wait to prove this point. I respond that, bad management or not, it's hardly the guests' fault. This pisses him off even more.

"Do you even *have* any food-and-beverage service experience?" he asks me angrily.

Sammy's day is a welter of dark rumination. Old injustices and ancient slights bubble up unbidden. Apropos of nothing, he tells me how in 1974 his grandfather chose not to help his son-in-law, Sammy's father, buy five New York taxi medallions at $5,000 per. Now they go for a quarter of a million bucks each. *A quarter of a million!* I return from lunch that day to find that Sammy has tried to tell Veronica, a preternaturally sweet towel girl who smiles all day long, how to do her job and she in turn has told him to go fuck himself. Later that afternoon, with the wedding now under way, he elbows a hotel guest to point out that the groom is "dressed like shit. He looks like a security guard."

Sammy works three jobs just to make his rent: here at the hotel from 10:00 to 6:00, at a restaurant from 7:00 to midnight, and the graveyard shift at a bar a few nights a week. At thirty-five, he is a good few years older than the rest of the regular pool staff. He has every right to be angry. But after a few hours with him it becomes clear that Sammy is as much the victim of cruel circumstance as he is of his own unerring capacity to misread situations and alienate others. During our orientation, we are plainly instructed to not overstep our duties. If, for example, we are asked for a restaurant recommendation, we are not, repeat not, to make one ourselves but to instead alert one of the concierges. Less than a second after this sentence has been spoken—the air around us still holding the gunpowder traces of the words—Sammy volunteers as how he'd "just send guests to Lincoln Road."

It's not like I can blame him. Lincoln Road does turn out to have a multitude of good restaurants. Where's the harm, really, in his suggesting one? I remember what it was like to feel powerless and invisible in a job I hated. My jaw ached from clenching my teeth all day. My mouth tasted as sour and acidic as if I'd crunched on a bottle of aspirin without water. Vivienne smiles patiently and suggests once more what she has just told us, and *again* Sammy says softly, not in defiance so much as in a kind of consoling lullaby to himself, "I'll send them to Lincoln Road." In honor of my old socialist summer-camp roots, I try never to side with management, but I have to concede that Sammy is incredibly exasperating to deal with. When I ask the general manager if a training session with the hotel's top brass is customary or if it was done for me as a writer, he responds with a pointed, "It wasn't for *your* benefit." Sammy has already worked room service at the hotel but got into many fights with his co-workers and was laid off. Pool Ambassador is his last chance.

He is one hundred percent right about one thing, though. Luiz really is a jerk. He dicks around making a frozen mojito, wasting time while saying twice during the process, "Damn, there's no one better than me." Even without extensive restaurant experience, and even though the guests don't seem to mind that the food takes as long as it does, all I want to do is grab Luiz by the front of his T-shirt and tell him to get on the fucking ball. It has been years since I spent my workday with other people. I had forgotten how quickly and deeply allegiances are formed, scapegoats are identified, and internecine backbiting becomes the governing drama of one's life. It is narcotically easy to fall back into those patterns. If I were to stay here even one day longer, I know I would be having whispered powwows in the housekeeping closet.

But I am not staying here one day longer. Too bad, just when it's getting nice out. South Beach has become chilly and overcast. I could work in weather like this. Only one lone couple sticks it out by the pool, huddled together on a chaise. They are possibly even doing it under the wrappings of several towels. Eventually, they give up and decamp to their room.

We pass the last two hours of our shift shivering by the bar. "There are days like this when there's no one here all day and still you have to stay 'til six," says towel girl Mavis. Pregnant and in her late teens, her mouth a glinting fretwork of braces. With little to do, she has spent the afternoon steadily nibbling her way through the cocktail garnishes. Her teeth are furred with pineapple fibers.

I finally tell my co-workers that this is my last day, that I only came down here to write about the experience. They don't much seem to care one way or the other. Their lack of reaction makes me wonder what exactly I came here to expose. There are more interesting jobs in the world, but heaven knows there are worse things than being bored in beautiful surroundings while servicing a surprisingly low-maintenance bunch of guests. One couple from Minnesota was downright delightful and even invited me out for supper. Over the course of three days, I don't witness a single moment's unpleasantness. No one forgets to say thank you or please, there is no "I'll have your job!" outrage in response to some imagined slight (and remember, I am the eyes and ears of the pool). After all, they're in a good mood—on holiday in a lovely hotel. It's not like I'm trying to mop under their feet in the OTB while they're on a losing streak. Then again, I have stood in beautiful restaurants in the greatest city in the richest country in the world and seen an obviously well-fed clientele behave as if it was being denied its last chance on earth for a meal. I have witnessed (only once and never again) the life-and-death feeding frenzy that is the Barneys warehouse sale. Maybe people are ruder at some of the more famous South Beach hotels, where the bars are crowded four deep and the guests have to yell to be heard while trying to look casual sitting on witty, uncomfortable poured-resin stools in the shape of blenders. If you have to constantly prove that you're cool enough to stay at a place, it increases the chances for toxic interactions. Nothing like being shown your low station in the pecking order to make you want to peck someone even lower. The fact that I am by no means the least attractive staff member here speaks volumes about the comparative egalitarianism of the Hiawatha.

I change for the last time, putting my uniform into the housekeeping bin for dry-cleaning (disgruntled employee habits die hard; I pocket the cute grosgrain belt). I head down the block to the drugstore to buy a razor and a post-work snack. Just ahead of me in the store is a young man: heavyset, acne, long black metal-rocker hair, oversized skate-punk T-shirt, shorts. He shuffles along, his flip-flops never breaking contact with the linoleum. I am caught in his patchouli vapor trail. He has a bag of Doritos in one hand, and in the other a stuffed alligator head. He carries it like a baseball mitt, with his fingers interlaced through the teeth of the open jaws. Approaching the register, he holds up the dusty reptile and asks, "How much is this?"

God knows you can buy some stupid, touristy shit along this commercial strip: shell-shaped ashtrays, leaping dolphins in porcelain and Plexiglas, towels printed with near-naked women whose round asses seem to be eating their own thongs, idiotic T-shirts printed with two arrows, one pointing up to your face that says "The Man" and another pointing down to your crotch that says "The Myth." And even though this fellow clearly found his treasure on the shelves of this Walgreens, I cannot imagine it's actually part of the store's inventory. More likely someone left it there. I'll go even further and posit that the kind of guy who would part with his hard-earned money for a poorly stuffed alligator head with cloudy amber glass eyes and cracking skin peeling up in places is also precisely the kind of guy who might absentmindedly leave it on the shelves of the place he went to buy his munchies.

The cashier attempts to find a bar code anywhere on the object, turning it this way and that in the red beam of his scanner. Eventually giving up, he raises it above his head and calls out over his shoulder into the refrigerated air of the store, "Price check on the alligator head." There is no surprise or amusement in his voice. It has been a long day.

MORNING IN AMERICA

I t's a lucky thing the metal content of glitter glue does not
set security wands to beeping. Otherwise the line stretching halfway down Forty-eighth Street would move even more
slowly. At least two hundred of us are waiting at six o'clock on
a Monday morning to get past the two men checking purses,
knapsacks, and the many homemade posters adorned with
balloon script, Day-Glo marker, and the careful application of
downloaded photographs of Matt Lauer. Once through security, we are corralled behind barricades outside the studio windows of the *Today* show.

Before Ground Zero achieved that quantum state of simultaneously being both part of the city and a talismanic outpost

of the rest of the country, the blocked-off street outside the *Today* show was a little piece of New York that all America could love, a destination for throngs who willingly line up to spend their early morning replicating an experience they have every day—watching television in their own homes—albeit in considerably less comfort.

It is springtime and the fake saplings on the *Today* show plaza are just coming into fabric blossom. The prime viewing spots are at the north end. There one can see into the studio itself. It is not the clearest view, it should be noted. There is a refractive amber Mylar-like sheeting on the windows. Still, it is a view. And it enables a mass-communications trifecta: one can see the show for real, watch it in real time on the monitor ten feet away, and—in a perfect world—be on a cell phone to friends and family back home to see if they can see you watching television on TV. But at not yet 7:00 a.m., the only people in the studio are the show's non-famous technicians. The monitors are off, showing an unchanging test pattern of the program's trademark rainbow logo, and the oddly insulting text, "Today Show / Generic Tease / Katie Couric." On the news zipper above the studio windows the words "Alan Greenspan" and "Enlarged Prostate" scudder by cheerfully in bright red pixels.

I take my place in what seems like *Today* Siberia, somewhere in the south middle. I probably won't get on television but it's still a very good location, placed as it is directly in line with the door where any of the show's hosts will come out.

And now we wait. A tall woman says into a cell phone, "All

I want is a date. A date that when he stands up I can see his eyes." Madonna's "Vogue" plays over the sound system, and more than one of the dozen late-adolescent boys in this largely female crowd start dancing and posing.

The telltale three notes of the NBC melody play. The show is about to begin and the crowd goes wild. A woman from Florham Park, New Jersey, holds up her poster with its (hopefully) inadvertently filthy math equation:

$$\frac{3 \text{ BOYS}}{+ 1 \text{ MOM}}$$
$$4 \text{ NYC}$$
$$\text{FUN}$$

They canceled their trip to Europe because of terrorism fears, so they are spending spring break in New York instead. I ask her which of the hosts she'd most like to meet. It is Al Roker, without question. Part of Roker's job by definition puts him into the most contact with the crowd. Factor into that that he was until recently all-too-humanly obese, offering the greatest surface contact possibilities just in pure metric terms, and I can sort of see why he is the live audience's hands-down favorite. Just then, Roker emerges like the godhead, walking up and down, vibing the crowd, who react like iron filings under a magnet. "Hiya!" he yells. People laugh as if he's made a joke.

"He's just so approachable," New Jersey Mom says.

Except that, inasmuch as we are behind police barriers and would be hauled off if we so much as attempted to breach them, Roker is exactly as approachable as Matt and Katie, which is not at all. Roker Time is good time, make no mistake, but it is brief time. He doesn't come out all that much, and the stretches in between his glorious manifestations are spent chatting and hanging out. It's a convivial party atmosphere as the loudspeakers announce upcoming stories about murdered Laci Peterson, the North Korea nuclear threat, and a CDC warning about SARS in Canada.

One group of girls tells me that, after this, they will be lining up for tickets to see *Montel,* and then *Conan O'Brien.* With any luck, they will not have to see anything of the city at all, their only glimpse of the skyline will be a plaster replica behind a desk.

Obviously not everyone is unmindful of where we are. A woman from Jessup, Iowa, two and a half hours by car from Des Moines, is visiting the show on her last morning of a five-day stay. She had come to New York to see her twenty-year-old son perform in a choir at Lincoln Center. She also saw *Thoroughly Modern Millie* and *Cabaret* ("A study in contrasts," she says). I ask if being here is the coolest part of her trip and she looks at me like I'm an idiot and says, slowly, enunciating, in case I had missed it the first time, "No, my son *singing at Lincoln Center* was the coolest part of my trip."

A foursome of young white guys from the Los Angeles area are standing around, blowing into cold hands, with no apparent or professed interest in the proceedings. Slim Shadys all of them: hooded sweatshirts, baseball caps, low-slung jeans, and foreheads spangled with constellations of acne. They drove all night from Ohio where one of their number is at college.

They've just arrived and will not be staying the night. "I want to know where the hookers are," says one. "I want to see Yankee Stadium," says another. A basketful of excited puppies, they are. Like a traffic cop, or Ray Bolger as the Scarecrow, I point my left hand westward ("Hookers . . .") and my right hand straight uptown (". . . and Yankee Stadium"). I resist the temptation to point out to them that we are standing not one hundred yards away from where Gene Kelly, Frank Sinatra, and Jules Munshin, playing sailors on leave in *On the Town*, faced a similar dilemma of how much ground to cover in a mere twenty-four hours. *Got to see the whole town / From Yonkers on down to the bay / In just one day!*

Although the studio is part of the frozen-in-amber deco perfection of Rockefeller Center, the *Today* show plaza is a completely generic space, evoking nothing. It's like one of those waterfront developments in every major North American city, where old warehouses are renovated and the big-shoulders brawn of their bygone days of industry is aped with Olde Worlde calliope wagons selling flavored popcorn, gourmet fudge, and stained-glass-window charms. We could be anywhere, except arguably the very city we are actually in.

Which is odd, because the goings on inside the studio itself can feel decidedly Gotham at times. Standing outside, we can hear the show, but not all that well as it turns out, and a lot of the throwaway stuff is lost in the buzz of the crowd. It might just be the segment I watch from home one morning, an appearance by a man named Steven Cojocaru, the fantastically flamboyant *Today* show style guy who looks like the love child of seventies rock god Steven Tyler and seventies Robert Altman goddess Shelley Duvall. When first we see him, they are freshly back from a commercial. The audio of American Idol Kelly Clarkson singing her treacly power ballad "A Moment Like This" plays. Cojocaru and Roker are cracking each other up on the sofa by lip-synching with outsize gestures; big, derisive, queeny fun. Cojocaru then launches into an anecdote about his flight east from LA where two fellow passengers were furtively going at it under some blankets, admitting no small personal bitterness over not being a member of the Mile High Club himself, tossing off the term like it was an organization as wholesome and widely known as 4-H.

Cojocaru has brought in a selection of accessories spawned by an upcoming movie, set in the Rock Hudson–Doris Day heyday. Proffering a feathered Audrey Hepburn hat, he tells news anchor Ann Curry to try it on. It's a large, raggedly elegant black zinnia of a thing. She dons it, and cracks up, saying, "I look like Angela Davis!" She does. More like an Angela Davis Muppet, actually. The cast and crew laughs a lot in the background. It's all witty and bitchy and knowing. We are catching them in a rare moment where they just don't care whether there is a general conversance out there with black sixties revolutionaries.

It's not a huge surprise that extremely highly paid New York media professionals might occasionally lapse into talking amongst themselves like extremely highly paid New York media professionals, but what makes it so funny is precisely the different frequency on which it seems to be playing, as inaudible as a dog whistle. It must be an eye-glazing comedown when Roker has to leave this blue-state cocktail party and go back outside through the magic portal to this little patch of America, to oversee a lawn-care demo.

THE DAYS OF the week I go to the show begin running together. On Friday I bump into Randy, a New York friend who is posing as an American. An American so very excited about the theatrical release that very day of MTV's spring break reality movie, that he is compelled to don shorts and a T-shirt and hold up a poster for said film. He is making $200. It seems like a waste of promotional-budget dollars, not simply because whatever might stick in the minds of viewers at home would at best be subliminal in the extreme but also because apparently the camera people tend to shy away from visibly commercially produced posters in favor of the personal variety. We chat and when the camera passes by, he hoists his foam-core sign and yells, with frat-boy zest, "Rock 'n' roll!"

At the beginning of the week, the impulse to be here had seemed like a failure of cognition; an inability to remember that just as we don't register the faces of the people sitting behind the Qualcomm advertisement—or behind Jack Nicholson, for that matter—at televised sporting events, why then should anyone in the crowd expect themselves to be noticed? But what initially looks to be a desire to be seen by millions turns out to be a wish to be seen by very few. A sign that reads HELLO MEDICINE HAT CANADA! is by definition aimed at a very narrow constituency. The contact sought with HI

GRANDMA AND PAPA. I MISS YOU. LOVE PRINCESS GABBY is intimate. Watching *Today,* even in public, is a very personal pursuit. The members of the crowd are not doing this for what could be characterized as the typical reality-television kind of attention: that disinhibited, oversexualized, bereft-of-pride behavior that makes people—whose parents are presumably still alive—allow themselves to be filmed having catfights while wearing thongs, or tucking into heaping plates of beef rectums (while wearing thongs). The simple act of standing, clothed, in the street with naught but a homemade sign seems almost Louisa May Alcott–sweet by comparison.

Almost. It is still television. A woman apparently bared her breasts one morning as the camera swept past her. And Roker, in one of the most juvenile and hilarious segments ever filmed anywhere, was the unwitting mark in a guerrilla prank staged by the Upright Citizens Brigade, the improvisational comedy troupe of cult renown. Founding member Matt Walsh, playing an Everyman named Alan, held up a sign that read MARRY ME KAREN. Roker picked him out of the crowd on what looked to be a perfect day in summer.

"I came to New York to raise awareness for Little Donny Disease, Magnimus-obliviophallocytus [a running gag in the Upright Citizens Brigade canon: a pseudo disorder essentially meaning being a kid with a huge schlong], and to propose marriage to a very beautiful woman."

The producers have gotten "Karen" (in reality Walsh's sister) on the line and Roker serves as interlocutor to the proposal, looking into the camera and asking her questions about herself and Alan. Walsh, the overanxious prospective groom, keeps interjecting.

"Settle down, or we're not going to do this," Roker warns, not idly.

The proposal is made and Karen consents. Alan goes apeshit with happiness, screaming "I love you Karen!" over and over. Fellow Upright Citizen Matt Besser has been standing in the background until this moment. He is here as Little Donny himself, he of the eponymous disorder. Sharing in Alan's happiness, he manages to move to the front of the crowd and begins to leap for joy. Roker has a look of mildest distaste on his face, and seems a little nonplussed by their excitement, but only a little. He understands the power the medium can have over people. When he finally registers the enormous pink prosthetic wang flopping out of the bottom of Little Donny's shorts, he realizes he's been had. Grace under pressure, he moves away from them, getting the penis out of camera range, saying only, "Okey-doke let's go . . . Oh my, no more coffee for that guy."

Little Donny aside, no one here seems to be confusing this with a means to their Big Break. During a brief foray outside, Katie Couric says, "Look at all these cute girls," just before they cut to commercial. Their mother beams, but doesn't hand over a mess of head shots. Her pleasure is as much about their *Today* stint being satisfyingly concluded. "That was perfect timing. Let's go get something to eat," she says, and they are out of there. It's 9:00 and Roker and Company have fulfilled their function as the city's highest-paid babysitters.

Today is just about the only place in New York City to take kids before 9:00 a.m., when the Pokémon store opens next door.

Even those in the crowd without youngsters in tow rush off to breakfast like it was a Fortune 500 board meeting. Our ranks begin to dwindle considerably. The last hour feels dogged and a good deal less festive standing in a group that gets smaller by the minute, on pavement strewn with trampled, abandoned signs (LIA AND JODEE. BEST FRIENDS IN NY FOR THE 1ST TIME AND LOVING IT!!).

Randy and I take a caffeine break at the Dean and Deluca facing the Plaza. A woman passes by outside the coffee shop. The window is a reflective surface with people behind it, and she illustrates the depth of her *Today* show Pavlovian conditioning by holding up the $8\frac{1}{2} \times 11$ color Xerox of her infant son, with the words HI SEAN on it. She mouths "My boy!" to those of us inside, pointing to her chest.

There is no more security to speak of when Randy and I return to positions to wait until the bitter end. We could now stand outside the studio naked with a shoulder-launched missile. It is down to a skeleton crew of thirty individuals. The already shaky sound on some of the monitors has been turned down significantly, others have been switched off completely. Technicians are striking the outdoor set. By 9:30, it's last call with the lights turned on. It's just sad.

A man in his late forties, salt-and-pepper hair, gray jogging suit, gold cross, approaches and asks Randy if he's planning on keeping his by now slightly bent spring break movie poster.

"I'm moving into a new apartment in Philly. I need artwork.

DON'T GET TOO COMFORTABLE

I'm here to see Katie. I sent her a white rose and a letter a while back."

He is lucid enough to understand that a response would be more than he could ever hope for. Not to worry, he has a contingency plan.

"I'm going to have my picture taken with the fake Katie." He produces a small flyer for something in the NBC building where one can pose with a life-size cutout, it seems.

"I have a thing for her. Like everyone else in the country," he confides. "I played college basketball. I broke my glasses." He is winding a thick rubber band around the bridge of the spectacles which are in two pieces, barely holding them together. "It's only a problem if I drive at night."

"How did you get here?" I ask.

"I drove."

Even he doesn't stick around for the very end. When the crypto-stalkers pull up stakes, it's definitely time to leave. The party is breaking up. By the time Katie Couric emerges to sign what can't total more than twelve autographs, the area is being slowly subsumed back into the life of the city, returning to being just more midtown sidewalk, the streets wrested away from the republic and reclaimed for the greatest city in the world as it is traditionally viewed from elsewhere: a heartless, tolerant island teeming with pushcarts, dusky immigrants, tycoons, chorines, homos, Jews, liberals, and, yes, hookers and Yankee Stadium.

MARTHA, MY DEAR

She was always an easy target. The jokes only escalated once she was hauled off to the clink. Imperious and controlling, people would say, her projects demanding the anal-retentive concentration of a Persian miniaturist. But now that she had been brought down for insider trading, the airwaves were abuzz with gags about her frantically knitting license-plate cozies and stitching rickrack borders onto the meager curtains in her cell. Let's watch her try to fend off the unwanted advances of the many tattooed bulldaggers who would claim her for their very own prison bitch.

I am not one for making predictions. She is still behind bars at the time of this writing. But I know in my heart that her reemergence will be an unmitigated triumph (the truism is dead wrong: there seem to be nothing *but* second acts in America). Mine is the unshakable faith of one who loves Martha Stewart and always has. I love her for a simple reason: she advocates mastery and competence over purchase. Martha Stewart has taught scores of people—and I'll go out on a limb here and call them women—the value of doing things for themselves. "How to make" almost always trumps "How to buy" in my book. (There are exceptions. I'm perfectly happy not to have to grind my own flour or blow my own lightbulbs.)

It was Martha Stewart, in fact, who made me realize that "art fag," the disparaging term I used to describe myself and my hobbies, was actually the same thing as being handy. (It was an epithet first hurled at me by some rough boys who walked by me late one night in Brooklyn when I was twenty-four years old. I didn't have the courage to yell back at them, "That's Arthur Fag to you!" I also didn't get it at the time that only a couple of fellow travelers could traffic in such subtle gradations of homosexual phenotypes. The average gay-basher doesn't know enough to call someone a Callas Queen, for example. Besides, "art fag" seemed so apt to describe what I was that I just adopted it as my own.)

I make stuff. Ersatz Joseph Cornell boxes, painted mirrors, that kind of thing. It's an itch, a compulsion that comes over me when I pass by a sidewalk piled with particularly good garbage, or when shopping for a table lamp, I see how little there really is to such an object and how much they're charging. Some people need to exercise every day, others don't feel complete without regular vacations. My salvation lies in time spent alone with an X-Acto knife and commercial-grade adhesive. I make stuff because I can't not make stuff.

During the act of making something, I experience a kind of blissful absence of the self and a loss of time. When I am done, I return to both feeling as restored as if I had been on a trip. I almost never get this feeling any other way. I once spent sixteen hours making 150 wedding invitations by hand and was not for one instant of that time tempted to eat or look at my watch. By contrast, if seated at the computer, I check my e-mail conservatively 30,000 times a day. When I am writing, I must have a snack, call a friend, or abuse myself every ten minutes. I used to think that this was nothing more than the difference between those things we do for love and those we do for money. But that can't be the whole story. I didn't always write for a living, and even back when it was my most fondly held dream to one day be able to do so, writing was always difficult. Writing is like pulling teeth.

From my dick.

I've often wondered what it must be like for one's work life to be a daily exercise in having that feeling of meditative pleasure. There is only one place where I can imagine that happening: the crafts department of *Martha Stewart Living* magazine. Considering that it is the destination of a pilgrimage, it's a bit anticlimactic to find myself in what could be any standard, fluorescent-lit corridor in any standard midtown building— aside from that sheaf of wheat, bound up and propped against the wall by the mail cubbyhole. It's not until I enter the office of Hannah Milman, who heads up the department, and see that every inch of every available surface, shelves and windowsills and radiators, is covered with an embarrassment of craft supplies—apothecary jars filled with seashells and beach glass, bags upon bags of quartz, polished oyster shells, beads, vintage rhinestones, spools of ribbon, silk and velvet flowers— that I know for sure that I have found a home of sorts. I feel both thrilled and envious, although the latter is misplaced. I've managed to amass a healthy trove of materials of my own over the years. At last inventory, the cupboards underneath my bookshelves, eighteen cubic feet of space, were packed solid with takeout soup containers full of tiny bulbs salvaged from old strings of Christmas lights, plastic fish, plastic horses, and some sinisterly cheerful plastic clown heads; seven boxes of Chinese-character flash cards; several dozen black Bakelite rotary-phone dials pulled from a Dumpster in front of the welfare office near my house; numerous packages of gold-foil Chinese joss paper; easily sixty tubes of acrylic paint and almost as many brushes; rhinestones; pearl buttons; a thick bundle of architectural balsa wood; a brick of gray-green plasticene; bulldog clips; pipe cleaners; a tin cracker box of multicolored golf tees, approximately 1,000; six stamp pads; rubber linoleum printing blocks with tubes of ink; five volumes of the 1952 *World Book Encyclopedia,* as well as six cracked, leather-bound books of a nineteenth-century technical dictionary; bindery-fabric sample books; three porcelain heads that I salvaged from some trash on Russian Hill in San Francisco well over ten years ago and have yet to make use of; and truest friend to crafters everywhere, assorted cans of polyurethane. (Glorious, glorious polyurethane! To your gorgeous fumes, a woozy hymn, with half the words missing! O resinous forgiver of countless mistakes, whose mirror-bright nacre confers authority, a glassy rime of reason to objects large and small! Hooray and huzzah, I wax for Minwax!)

Still looking around in wonder, my eyes light upon Hannah Milman's collection of eggs. It is the kind of comprehensive assortment of species, sizes, and colors that the good agents at the fish and wildlife service might like to know about. The eggs, many dozen in number, are all empty and clean. I ask her if she blew them out herself, a task which, after the fourth or fifth egg, starts to give one the mother of all headaches. Everyone pitched in, she says. It was for a feature the magazine did about how to make your own Fabergé egg. She shows me one of the finished products, created in-house. The fragile shell has been sawed open with the tiny bit of a Dremel drill, its two perfect halves edged in narrow gold brocade, hinged, and lacquered a pale imperial blue. Inside is a tiny velvet pillow on which a pearl rests like a baby.

It is lovely and useless. I don't really go in for homemade versions of evil czarist frippery, but I tamp down my reservations by repeating to myself what She Herself taught me: these eggs require easily as deft a hand, probably more so, as it takes to refinish a cabinet on the super-butch *This Old House*. At most, it's a difference of degree, not kind. Handy, handy, I am handy.

HANNAH LEADS ME down the hall to the main workroom. It is not a large space by any means. There is a central table and a work surface running along two walls. On the floor-to-ceiling shelves are clear plastic storage boxes of still more supplies. The project currently under way is traditional Polish Christmas ornaments. Stalks of that selfsame wheat from the hallway are being soaked, folded, twisted, braided, and tied into an endless variety of shapes by half a dozen of Martha's elves. Despite the humility of the materials, there is nothing simple about the ornaments as they are dusted with differing shades of brilliant metallic mica powder, an incredibly toxic substance that has the young man using it—the only man working here, in fact, albeit curiously named Meghan—wearing a double-filtered gas mask. The crafters are all hunched over their small wheaten garlands and wreaths. I ask them if they ever experience that wonderful feeling of absence.

A woman named Kelly says, "When you're making something, you're in a different state. You go into a deep level of concentration, to the point where you're not self-conscious anymore, it's just flowing out of you."

It's fairly amazing that she has used these words unprompted, because the actual name for the state of mind that she is describing is "flow." It's a term coined by Mihaly Csikszentmihalyi, a University of Chicago–trained psychologist. In trying to codify those moments that give our life purpose, that elevate the consciousness and add complexity to the self, Csikszentmihalyi interviewed athletes, chess players, artists, rock climbers, and found that all of them, when engaged in the act of their choosing, spoke of reaching a level of engagement that is completely unselfconscious, removes them from their everyday worries, and alters their sense of time.

"The biggest challenge for us is that you have to have insta-flow," Kelly continues. "You *have* to make things. You don't have a choice. That's what you're paid for."

My flow would fly right out the window at the first sign of external pressure. And that pressure here is a constant. Moreover, it seems more often than not to have to do with Christmas, Thanksgiving, or Easter. I just don't care about the holidays enough. I'm also a little hung up on functionality. I try to not make stuff that is solely decorative. And I'm sort of im-mune to the spotless, relentlessly American Martha Stewart aesthetic, a kind of family-quilt-inherited-from-the-grand-mother-who-never-had-to-run-from-the-Cossacks *goyishkeit* that really isn't my thing. There are reasons beyond my lack of tal-ent and training for why I could never work here.

And yet I still feel a great sense of commonality with these women. I ask them if they think the world divides into people who don't make stuff and people who do. They answer diplo-matically, like social workers, saying how everyone has their own special creativity. They think that I'm trying to catch them out in some snobbery, to claim membership in some exclusive group. But I'm talking about something as value neutral as double-jointedness. The inability to look at something without wanting to somehow make it into something else, a compul-sion completely separate from aesthetics or talent. I try a different tactic. I ask if they've ever passed by the garbage of Duggal Photo, a processing lab in the Flatiron district. The trash at Duggal almost always has something good: pristine black cardboard, which would cost a lot to buy in a store, or some very nice acetate or clean foam core. Suddenly they know exactly what I'm talking about. Just thinking about it makes their eyes light up like the Cratchett children on Christmas morning.

Actually, there is a much clearer marker by which to divide the population: between the people who make things, and the people who receive the things we make. Staying up late exploring one's obsession of the moment is one thing, foisting the product of those obsessions upon friends and loved ones is something else entirely.

Giving someone an art project might appear very generous on the surface, but in another sense it's an act of bullying. More than a store-bought gift, it's an attempt to curate someone else's taste. You're also consigning them to the task of having to take care of your work. It's a bit like leaving a baby on their doorstep. After the initial amazement at its profound beauty, it simply becomes a liability. I have made and given away easily twenty years' worth of things. Some of the recipients have moved almost that many times. Others have died, gotten divorced, or been widowed. I have made things out of food—polyurethaned food, but food nonetheless.

"I was doing a lot of mushroom prints, and everyone got one for their birthday that year," muses one of the women. "Actually, you know, come to think of it, I haven't seen a lot of those up. I wonder what happened to them."

I'm doubtful that much of the stuff I've made is still around. A year on the shelf and then out to the rubbish heap or Goodwill seems like a perfectly suitable statute of limitations to me, but one can never know the mind of another person. I have almost no idea what has happened to a lot of the stuff I've made. I try to track down some of the objects.

For my friend Deb's thirtieth birthday, I made her a box, painted pastel pink and tiled all over in Necco wafers. On the inside is pasted a sticker from the Women's Health Action Mobilization, an activist group she was involved with. SUPPORT VAGINAL PRIDE, it says. She has it close at hand when I call about it. That it would be within easy reach in a studio apartment is no surprise. But that she would still have it at all after so many years with such limited living space kind of is.

"I keep it because it's pretty and silly. It's frilly and girly and covered in these ballerina cake-toppers. It's not my style, and that's a joke that you and I share. It's something I have to explain. It's what people at Lillian Vernon might call a conversation piece."

For the most part, the friends I call have kept the things I made. Sometimes they go missing, but there always seems to be a reason beyond mere neglect. Case in point, my friend Margaret, now settled in Boston. I have to remind her of the mirror I made for her and her then-husband Lander's wedding. She has no memory of it.

"He probably has it. He made a big grab for the stuff, *but I got the car!*" she jokes. After a pause, she says, "You know what, I'm suddenly remembering the mirror. We hung it up. I think

he took it! I think his new wife's name is Marta, so he probably just twisted the letters around. That's funny, just thinking
about it, *He took that mirror David gave me,* gets me mad at
him. I haven't thought about him in years. Talk about the
power of repression."

Talk about the power of repression, indeed. I have made
Margaret remember something she hadn't really wanted to,
and she turns around and does the same thing to me. She has
kept a T-shirt that I painted for her when we were in college.
Just hearing her describe it makes me cringe.

"I see it every day. It's very eighties. It's a portrait of someone. Big beautiful eyes, and sensuous lips. The man of your
dreams? It's the romantic David I know."

The romantic David she knows. That's the problem. If
forced, I suppose I can remember the *kind* of T-shirt Margaret
is talking about, but horror at what must have been my technical limitations coupled with my youthful infractions of taste
prevent me from being able to conjure up an actual image.
The mark of a true friend is someone who remembers you
from sophomore year and doesn't hold it against you that you
painted a huge copy of van Gogh's sunflowers on the wall of
your dorm room, for example. But you don't expect friends to
keep the artifacts of your shame. Unless, of course, you've
been bossily distributing the evidence for years yourself. It had
never occurred to me that the latent content of the things I've
made would serve as a visual record of my state of mind, more
oblique and therefore more telling than any diary I might have
kept. The thing that Margaret described in particular sounds

like such a bald and unguarded glimpse into the yearning of the hayseed I used to be, that I wish she had thrown it away. I remain shocked that she didn't, seeing as how she's indicted just by association. It means that she, too, was once—I hate even to type the word—young.

THERE WAS A photo spread when I was very young in *Life* magazine, I think. It was a series of pictures of an autistic girl. It must have been one of the very first glimpses into the disorder. In one photograph, the girl is standing, her back against the kitchen wall. Her arms are out from her sides at forty-five-degree angles, and her hands are a blur, like hummingbirds. Her face is a mask of utter serenity. The caption mentioned that, according to her parents, she found great enjoyment and relaxation in this action. It made perfect sense to my seven-year-old brain. I, too, had felt that pleasurable sense of isolation, that calming silence, the deep and regular breath when I moved my hands that quickly, whirring over objects. It wasn't until many years later that I found out that "autistic" wasn't just some alternate spelling of "artistic."

IT'S A LOVELY moment when I watch people unwrap the things I make, but I don't much care if they keep them out of any sense of artistic ego. And I really don't want to think about the object overstaying its welcome, or somehow becoming the physical reminder of the contempt or pity in which I am held. Here's how it would go: thirty years hence, our connection long since sundered, these people are sitting around with their families, the gift in question is spotted, and all of a sudden time melts away and I am conjured up on a wave of pitying laughter that washes over the room. Their grown children lean over to *their* children and say, "Listen up, you'll like this story," and then a tale will unfold of the fellow who "made us this thing and came to our wedding and got *so* drunk. I wonder whatever happened to him?" they will ask, not really wondering and caring even less. I had thought that the more controlling position was donor, not recipient. And it is, until the moment you give the thing away, and then, as with most everything in this world, it is out of your hands.

I CAN'T GET IT FOR YOU WHOLESALE

In *Mahogany*, Diana Ross, playing the world's greatest super-model-turned-designer, has stayed entirely too long at the fair and is sick to death of all the falsehood and decadence. Her affair with mercurial photographer Tony Perkins is on the skids. At a party, surrounded by her brittle, beautiful, shallow friends, she drips melted wax onto her torso, laughing mirth-lessly all the while. I watched rapt, having been taken to see it by my best friend Mark Satok and his family. That same year, while handing hors d'oeuvres around my parents' living room, I said to a friend of the family, "That's a nice dress. Is it an Albert Nippon?" It was a rhetorical question. I already knew that it was. I was ten years old.

My knowledge of fashion hasn't really advanced much in the intervening thirty years. At this point, I am less informed than the average *InStyle* reader. Still, I have been chosen to go to Paris to cover the couture collections for a fashion magazine, armed with little more than a notebook and my febrile, movie-fueled imagination that keeps on sending the same derivative scenario sloshing across my brainpan: an impoverished seamstress, her fingers bloody from hours of painstaking needlework, is being dressed down by an outraged couturier.

"I asked for camellias. These are not camellias," he says, ripping out the stitches. "Do it again." He flings the garment at her, an errant bugle bead catching her right in the eye. She weeps softly. The designer's teacup poodle, Sal Mineo, yaps agitatedly throughout.

In Paris, I will learn a great deal over the course of the week. I will see the reality behind the glamorous façade. I will learn about cut and sewing and artistry. Most of all, I will learn that the old pronouncement attributed to the Duchess of Windsor, Wallis Simpson—one of the world's worst people ever—is, not surprisingly, wrong. It is distinctly possible to be both too rich and too thin.

The boondoggle starts before I even get there. The magazine is flying everyone business class. The front cabin before takeoff is a flirty cocktail party in full swing, but the joviality conceals a slightly nicked sordidness. The sofa is starting to show some wear—the upholstery on the arms and back is shiny and worn—and the seat belts between the cushions and heavy metal bolts securing it to the floor of the aircraft kind of ruins the *Playboy After Dark* effect. Ditto the bar stools, which taper down to industrial-sized rivets in the carpet. It gives the place a minimum-security-prison feel, as though it was designed to withstand some potential upset over and above mere flight. Someone getting liquored up, breaking a flight attendant's arm, and defecating on the drinks cart, for example. I scan the crowd for a likely candidate. As we begin to taxi, all those felicities of groundedness—the vase of flowers on the bar, the magazines fanned just so on the coffee table, the shining racks of gleaming glassware—are whisked away and stowed. The speakeasy converting to a revival meeting moments before the cops rush in.

The first-class purser, a very handsome young man, comes by and kneels beside me. "Hi, I'm Nigel. I've been so busy I haven't had a chance to come and say hello!" he says with a tone of incredulity, not that he should be busy but that it should prevent him from greeting me, *me,* after all we've been through. This kind of friendly service from someone as painfully good-looking as Nigel just makes me feel shy and unworthy. I barely glance at him when I mutter hello. He probably thinks I'm an asshole, although he couldn't be friendlier as he hands me an extensive menu. I can order anything from it at any time in as much quantity as I like. It's all about unchecked plenty here. I probably won't avail myself. Given the fact that I'm somewhat obsessed with food, eating in front of other people is always somewhat embarrassing, like being caught in an illicit moment of arousal. And I am paranoid about spilling. My usual uniform of T-shirt, jeans, and sneakers will not do at the shows, apparently, and in order to limit my luggage to a carry-on, I have boarded the plane in my suit. I will have to wear it the next day, and many days after that, too, so I am trying to stay wrinkle and stain free. I sit up straight, dressed like a mortician, rigid as a corpse in what would otherwise be a really commodious seat.

At about 3:00 a.m., I am startled by a great yawp of laughter from a man who has been drinking way too much. In his midsixties and dressed in the charcoal-gray fleecy pajamas provided for him by the airline, he is trying to make time with a young woman with a spiky bleached 'do. This might be his lucky night, because she slouches toward him and loudly confides, "I thought I'd sleep, but I guess I'll just get pissed instead."

A flight attendant steps forward and tells them that she has bad news, the bar is closed. Unfortunately, international law dictates that they have to stop serving four hours before landing, she explains. The man is too drunk to call her out on this patent lie. The blonde seems not to care and staggers back to her seat, her manifest destiny of skankiness suspended for the moment. Scanning the man's face and body language and persuaded that he is not belligerent, the flight attendant walks away, leaving him standing there still trying to formulate his response.

MY FIRST ACT of rationalization: I will be on a very steep learning curve, attending multiple shows each day, all in different places around Paris, a city I do not know. The driver they have given me for the entire week is really a necessity, not a luxury. Olivier drives fashion people almost exclusively, so on the trip from the airport he gives me a quick survey of the differences between couture and ready-to-wear. Some of the stuff I already know, like how couture is made to order, while ready-to-wear is produced in factory multiples. Other stuff I don't, such as how proper couture shows traditionally have fifty garments per collection. They begin with daytime wear, move into evening, and generally end with a wedding dress. Also, when they say that couture garments are entirely handmade, they mean every single aspect: the cutting and edging of buttonholes, the sewing of seams, the lining of sleeves. None of it can make use of anything more automated than a needle and scissors.

I ask how much the dresses cost. Olivier cannot give me a definitive answer. In fact, the entire week I am there, no one can. Estimates are anything from $20,000 to $100,000. The main thing to remember, he tells me, is that even though much of couture is nonsense, its essential unwearability doesn't stop "the Jews of fashion," as he calls them, from coming to shows season after season with their sketch pads to copy and produce commercial knockoffs.

Dropping me off for a power nap before my first appointment, Olivier warns me about my hotel. "It is very chic and the people who work there are very beautiful, so if you want something, you must ask three times." The lobby is a close, red seraglio of a place. Paisley atop paisley, the air heavy with the scent of the hotel's trademark candle, available for purchase, along with the hotel's apparently world-famous dance-mix CD playing on the sound system. Even midmorning on a workday, the place is full of perfect specimens of both sexes, guests and staff alike, draped bonelessly over the furniture. A harem of Dalí's rubber clocks with all the time in the world.

Toadlike, I hop over to the front desk and check in. Into the tiny elevator, along a dark red hallway that seems to be illuminated by nothing more than lit cigarettes, and into a room that would be a highly coveted one-bedroom apartment in New York. I have a sitting room with a tasseled damask sofa, a passageway with walnut-doored closets leading to a bedroom, and beyond that a bathroom with a claw-footed tub. I count no fewer than three vases of roses. All the magazine people are staying here, presumably in digs just as sumptuous, except for the editors in chief, who are staying around the corner at the Ritz, which is even fancier. Looking out to the central courtyard filled with statues, I realize that I have crossed the parliament floor. I used to identify with the downtrodden seamstress in that story I told myself, but I have now thoroughly joined the ranks of the imperious monstrocracy.

WE TRAVEL AS a delegation that includes the magazine's editor in chief, fashion director, and Natasha, a beautiful, funny, intelligent, aphoristic Englishwoman who works in the publication's Paris office. In addition to attending the shows themselves, we go on studio visits where the conceit of each collection is explained. Our first appointment is at Christian

DAVID RAKOFF

Dior. John Galliano, the house designer, is a runty, sexy Brit dressed in a dark wool waistcoat with no shirt and a pair of khaki clam diggers slung low on his hips, his gray underpants showing. He greets us, myself included, with incredible warmth, kisses on both cheeks for the ladies.

His show will kick off the entire couture week the next day. The place is a buzz of activity with about thirty people going about their business. Some folks are decorating Day of the Dead masks at a table, a gorgeous black model is having green-and-gold reptile scales painted directly onto her naked torso, a seamstress is putting the finishing touches on bridesmaid's dresses being worn by two little girls who walk the length of the room unsmiling. They turn, and everyone applauds.

The walls are plastered with photographs torn from books and magazines, postcards, small objects, pages of text, and scribbled illustrations. Galliano's various inspirations. He caused an uproar a few seasons ago by showing clothing made to look like crumpled newspaper. Trivializing homelessness, some reports said. The conceptual springboard of this collection is a quote from a 1909 letter Freud wrote to Jung: " 'Recently I glimpsed an explanation for the case of fetishism. So far it concerns only clothing and shoes. But it is probably universal.' Mr. Dior was one of the first fetishistic designers," he tells us, leading us through the dramatic structure of the show. "There's the primal scene, with a little bit of *Rules of the Game,* seeing Mommy with the chauffeur, along with a bit of *Mädchen in Uniform* thrown in. Then we enter the world of the subconscious, trying on Mommy's lipstick. An alligator eats Mommy or is Mommy the alligator? The nanny turns into a rocking horse. And clowns! Because they still freak me out."

It doesn't feel like he's making it up as he goes along to justify the clothes, ascribing logic after the fact. Looking at the garments, it really does seem like he's mined an idea and riffed on it to its extremities. He has to do this twice a year.

"It's all savage," says Galliano's right hand and muse, a young woman with a sleek cap of white-blond hair, wearing what looks like a brown knit sling on her arm, "but the shoes match the handbag match the skirt."

Despite the loud military drums alternating with Bernard Herrmann's Hitchcock scores playing on the stereo, and all the work there is still left to do by the following morning, it's very calm and good-natured here. No one is raising their voice, people are smiling. We go upstairs to the ateliers. There are two of them: *l'atelier de flou,* for the looser unstructured garments, like evening wear, and *l'atelier tailleur,* for suits and such. Both are white and very clean, more surgery than Santa's workshop. Everyone is in a lab coat. There is a lot of embroidery being finished. Someone is completing an image of Marie Antoinette on a farthingaled skirt, there are elaborate Chinese peonies on a saffron silk dress, silver Mexican milagros are being secured to a hem. "Sublime" (*Soo-bleem*), says Natasha to one of the artisans.

We walk out into the Paris twilight. I've resolved to stay vigilant about the precise moment all the rarefaction and theater start to seem old hat or uninteresting. I am not bored yet.

———

GRAY LIGHT POURS through the sloping glass roof of Jean-Paul Gaultier's studio in a low building that sits off the street in a courtyard. It calls to mind those nineteenth-century photographs of Rodin at work. Like Galliano, Gaultier—dressed in what is his trademark Jean-Genet-rough-trade-sailor-lookin'-for-a-handjob-and-a-punch-up manner—greets us with exceeding friendliness. Tables are piled high with bolts of netting. A boom box encrusted with aquamarine rhinestones pours forth a tinny radio broadcast. On the floor are laid out multiple pairs of mules all lined in rabbit, looking like Meret Oppenheim's famous surrealist fur-lined teacup.

All I know about JPG are his costumes for Madonna videos and the Peter Greenaway film *The Cook, the Thief, His Wife, and Her Lover.* There are no cone bras on display. Instead, Gaultier has been experimenting with the way images can be broken down into their constituent dots, like in newspapers. He holds up a salt-and-pepper tweed dress and as we step back, the face of the singer Edith Piaf appears. There is a dress sewn out of square pixels in shades of green velvet that turns into the kissing faces of Bogey and Bacall in *To Have and Have Not.* It is incredibly cool. Gaultier jokes that he should offer to digitize the face of the client onto whatever dress they buy. "That's real couture."

He takes us up to the atelier where, just as at Dior, things feel industrious without being frenetic. We stand over a chocolate-brown velvet dress being beaded with an image of Pigalle, the louche Times Square of Paris and home to the

Moulin Rouge. Leading us out, Gaultier stops at the door and turns around, addressing the men and women preparing his collection, and says with great courtliness and sincerity, "Merci, mesdames et messieurs."

STEEL BARRICADES HAVE been set up outside the École des Beaux-Arts, site of the Dior show. Behind them are the gawkers and fashion groupies gazing covetously at what looks like old home week for the people pouring into the space. The hall is the size of a train station and its glass roof has been louvered shut, rendering the place very dark and very red, and heating up rapidly from the crush of bodies. The soundtrack is an extended loop of plinky piano punctuated by the occasional whip crack, followed by orgasmic moaning. I look around for a fire exit.

Crowd control and general ushering is handled by *les cravates rouges*, a suspiciously handsome cadre of young men who wear red ties and travel from venue to venue like the pope's Swiss Guard. Although an ignoramus, I am here with an influential magazine, so I have a very good seat. I am never farther back than the second row. The front row is reserved for high-ranking industry folk, the famous, and the clients, those fabulously wealthy Ladies who actually buy and wear the dresses. They are a small group and, as far as I can tell, not related, but it is extraordinary how many of them look as alike as sisters. Perhaps it is their universal whippet thinness, the shared knife-blade noses, or the full, pillowy mouths. Or is it the look of constant surprise in their unnaturally wide, unblinking eyes? The Ladies are an uncanny cluster of genetic coincidence, with the exception of their newest and youngest member—a sullen twentysomething Russian with a penchant for short denim miniskirts who is escorted everywhere by her much older benefactor, a raven-haired magnate with a face like raw chicken.

People are kissing friends hello, pointedly avoiding others, and scanning the crowd for celebrities, although one doesn't have to scan very hard. The arrival of anyone famous is heralded by a sudden turbulence in the waters of the room. Little crowdlets of piranhalike photographers jockeying for position form spontaneously. People speculate who might be at the center of the cluster of lights. This week, the immediate and unvarying first answer is always a hopeful "Gwyneth?" She has not shown up at Dior, but Elle MacPherson has, as have Steven Spielberg and his wife, who is sporting a bosom of unyielding, architectonic prominence.

Although it's as dark as my hotel in here, many of the women keep their sunglasses on. Why is that, I ask Natasha. "Well, darling, suppose your husband has just announced he's taken a mistress and you cried just a little bit on your way over."

The show begins after an hour of waiting, which I will find is a fairly standard interval. Even though I have seen the clothes the day before, I haven't seen them in their intended order. Costumes are augmented with props like handcuffs or mouths gagged with shiny red tape. Taken as a whole, there really is a narrative of sexual trauma. In Galliano's lubricious take on the haute bourgeoisie, there are a lot of dirty girls and boys in service. The chambermaids flash their panties, the nurses show leg while brandishing big hypodermic needles, and the filthy chauffeurs are constantly on the brink of running out of gas in the middle of nowhere. The actress Marisa Berenson plays a composed matriarch in mauve; another woman in an embroidered silk kimono carries a huge wooden cross; Marie Antoinette canters down the runway with a huge windup key protruding from her back. All told, the parade lasts seventeen minutes.

Consensus is that the show was a success. I surf along with the crowd as people climb up on the runway and make their way backstage to congratulate Galliano. Posted on a wall I see the last-minute instructions to the models. They should remember to embody fully the roles they have been given, whether proud and elegant or severe and kinky. Finally, it says, "Be confident, you're beautiful!" Anywhere else, this would seem an empty self-help exhortation to focus on one's inner worth and to let it shine forth. Here, it is merely a statement of fact.

Actually, the striking thing about the runway models is that they're not that beautiful close up. What they do possess— and what contributes to the sense of occasion—is presence, at least part of which can be chalked up to having mastered the Walk: that characteristic slouching, ball-bearing-hipped sashay. Not long prior to my arrival in Paris, I learned how to track animals at a wilderness survival camp. One of the methods used for identifying a species' prints is in calculating the animal's straddle, the distance of the hoof or paw out from an imaginary central line. Only one species has negative straddle, where the feet actually crisscross over that line: cats. And runway models. And absolutely no one has better negative straddle than Carmen Kass, an Estonian—again, hugely successful, not that gorgeous—who walks with such a percussive rimshot swagger and an unsmiling Clint Eastwood look that it just dares the photographers to go ahead and shoot her.

No mean feat to stare down that anarchic mass of arms, cameras, and flashbulbs at the end of the runway. A lot of the models play a pissing contest with the photographers, refusing to slow down to give them a more sustained pose to shoot, or a view of the back of the dress. The girls simply keep walking, ignoring the collective, impassioned pleas to "Stoppe!" or "Geau bacques!"

The photographers are a vocal mob. Once, when one of them was denied entry to a Gaultier show, they walked out en masse and had to be mollified with a champagne reception. If things are late in getting started, it is they who begin the rhythmic applause. They are also audibly appreciative. At the Ungaro show, one of the model's breasts pops out from her gauzy top, if "pops" can really be used to describe the movement of something so subdued in structure and size. After almost a week of seeing barely concealed and sometimes completely exposed tits, they still hoot and holler. The model covers up and smiles at them with indulgent exasperation. The honors student secretly pleased with the attentions of the cool kids in the back of the class.

———

A SIGN OVER the door at the Chanel offices has a quote, *La création n'est pas démocratique.* I take that as my cue to sink into the background, perfectly content to be invisible enough to overhear, "Belts. Think belts!" which garners a thoughtful "Yes . . ." then a pause, and a "Why belts now?" asked with all the inquiring seriousness of a young Siddhartha seeking enlightenment.

All of the designers I have met up to this point have been very nice, although upon being introduced to Karl Lagerfeld, he looks me up and down and dismisses me with the not super-kind, "What can you write that hasn't been written already?"

He's absolutely right, I have no idea. I can but try. The only thing I can come up with at that moment is that Lagerfeld's powdered white ponytail has dusted the shoulders of his suit with what looks like dandruff but isn't. Also, not yet having undergone his alarming weight loss, and seated on a tiny velvet chair, with his large doughy rump dominating the miniature piece of furniture like a loose, flabby, ass-flavored muffin overrisen from its pan, he resembles a Daumier caricature of some corpulent, inhumane oligarch drawn sitting on a commode, stuffing his greedy throat with the corpses of dead children, while from his other end he shits out huge, malodorous piles of tainted money. How's that for new and groundbreaking, Mr. L.?

THERE SEEM TO be two varieties of applause. The first is the appreciation of peers, professionals who clap for beautiful sewing, for the outrageously good swing of a caviar-beaded skirt. The second kind of applause comes from the Ladies, whose polite ovations greet outfits they feel they could actually wear. At the older designers' shows, like Oscar de la Renta for Pierre Balmain, they busily make checkmarks on their lists when the gold silk skirt and jacket trimmed in parrot-green fur parades by, their eyes wide with soon-to-be-satiated hunger and relief. *Oh, thank God I don't have to put this $20,000 back into the bank!* But the shows that skew younger can be confounding experiences for them. Donatella Versace—looking like a small bondage sausage, a tight and meaty cylinder of bronze flesh packed into black leather—makes her victory lap after her show of sleazy dresses. The long-anticipated Gwyneth, looking very pretty but far too blond, and Jennifer Lopez and her boyfriend-at-the-time Sean Combs, seated across the runway are all very enthusiastic, but the Ladies sit on their hands for the most part. At Alexander McQueen's show for Givenchy they find even less worth contemplating.

We are all driven to La Défense, the area outside of central Paris where they have crowded their modern skyscrapers, thereby preserving the historic perfection of the city itself. McQueen wants to show clothing that blends high and low, "like a downtown New York party where uptown people go and mix." We are in a huge arena space with seating on four sides. In the center is a small brick pavilion, with the Givenchy name spray-painted on its sides. Two women saunter in clutching bottles in paper bags, and knock on the door. A man holding a drink exclaims in joyous greeting and pulls them in and the door closes. Silence.

We sit a moment briefly doing nothing before the walls lower to become part of the floor plan of an apartment filled with revelers. I am sitting directly facing the bathroom. The music blares, a go-go boy—more of a go-go man, really—very admirably makes no effort to suck in his stomach as he stumble-dances around in a pair of tight white shorts. The models come in, show their dresses to all four sides of the audience and then just join the party, bobbing affectlessly to the music and having what appear to be real drinks. One young woman comes in wearing a wig that looks like a square boxwood topiary and sits down on the toilet, another wears a coat of multicolored rabbit-fur sausages and a Penelope Pitstop helmet in avocado. It's all bleary and blunted and strung-out.

"So *irritating*," drawls one of the more prominent Ladies, a dowager with hair coiffed into an unmoving iron-gray clamshell. They make their way back to their waiting cars, walking across a stark round plaza that looks, appropriately enough, like the amphitheater in the movie *Logan's Run* where they killed all the people over thirty.

Yves Saint Laurent must be a welcome antidote after such a large dose of muzzy, druggy youthfulness, despite the designer's own very public history with chemicals. His show is the pinnacle of couture week. It is the only time people are asked to turn off their cell phones. The acknowledged master, he has announced his imminent retirement and people are gathering reverently around the hospital bed. Across the aisle sits Tom Ford, the young tyro to whom he is handing the ready-to-wear reins. There is actor George Hamilton, tandooried to a fare-thee-well, and beside him Lauren Bacall, looking not much older than the digitized green-velvet image of her on that Gaultier dress. The designer's good friend, the eerily preserved Catherine Deneuve, is front and center. Who knew *The Hunger,* her film about ageless vampires, was a documentary?

I wish I could describe the clothes, but somewhere around outfit number sixty-four of a staggering ninety-two, the heat in the un-air-conditioned room starts to get to me and it is all I can do to stave off the twin impulses to pass out or throw up on the poor women from the *International Herald Tribune* in front of me. I would have to cross the runway to get out of this ballroom, so I am reduced to trying to strip down to my T-shirt without anyone noticing, while blotting myself with a handkerchief I am rolling into a cylinder and dipping into my Evian with my head between my knees.

Evidently, I missed something historic. People are ramped up as we emerge from the ballroom. André Leon Talley of *Vogue* gushes, "Hats are old and he even made a hat look decorative. Of course you would have to be at a wedding in northern Germany to wear it, but still!"

Natasha, my English colleague, is transported. "God, what beautiful cutting!" she exclaims. "You know, they offered me a present for my wedding and I'm sure they thought I was going to ask for a bridal gown but I didn't. I just wanted *un smoking.*" (Pronounced smoh-KEENG, it's Saint Laurent's emblematic androgynous dinner jacket for women.) "It was being fitted for me and I said to the man who was cutting it—whose name was Jean Pierre and of course I *loved* him because my husband's name is Jean Pierre—I said, 'Jean Pierre, this garment is so beautifully cut it could support an army!' You know it was just like *this*." She demonstrates by touching the pads of her thumbs to the pads of her middle fingers, and pulling down— an almost Bollywood-looking gesture. The goddess Siva lowering a window shade. "Just like that. *So* beautiful, you know?"

But I don't know. I don't know any of it. My shirt front is transparent from the more than half a bottle of water with which I have doused myself and I am feeling incredibly shaky and I no longer have the capacity to articulate anything. I like pretty things, I suppose, and things that make me feel stuff, but if there were a gun at my head at this moment, I couldn't elaborate on that thought. Suddenly it all feels beyond my grasp. My aesthetic comprehension of the entire century— why the Jasper Johns American-flag painting is so good; why it should trouble me that artists like Damien Hirst don't do the actual physical making of their art, while it doesn't bother me that Frank Gehry isn't laying his own titanium siding; why the directors of the French New Wave spawned generations of cineastes who consider *Kiss Me Deadly* a masterpiece while I just can't bear that movie—it's all running through my fingers like sand. All my fancy education and artfully crafted cant can't help me now. I am feeling linear and literal and must not be mentally taxed with anything more difficult than the sledgehammer subtle symbolism of, say, a butterfly landing on a coffin. Where was I? Oh, that's right: I like pretty things. Tell me about the rabbits, George.

It has finally happened. I am tired of it all. If I have to look at more beautiful clothing or have another conversation about beautiful clothing or feign amusement at any more adoring anecdotes about what a *caution* one of the Ladies is because, when being interviewed, she insisted upon a glass of straight vodka because, as she said, "I don't drink water—fish fuck in it," I will start shooting. I am oversated with perfection, a deadened, gouty feeling. I want to go home and clean my bathroom, or anybody's bathroom, for that matter.

Perhaps I can find the equivalent of a dark room and a washcloth for my forehead by forgoing the crowds and standing backstage for the Lacroix show. Things are extremely mellow when I arrive at 4:30 for a show scheduled to begin at 4:30. The models, incredibly young up close and also arboreally tall, still sit around in street clothes although their makeup has been applied and their hair has been lacquered back into attenuated bubbles like the world's most gorgeous malignant brain tumors. They have split up into their respective language groups: Portuguese, Russian, English.

I talk to Erin O'Connor, a sweet dark-haired willow tree of a girl who is apparently quite famous. She lets me touch the dry spaghetti of her hair. She was a ballet dancer for eleven years. "This is much easier. No daily practice, no injuries." In addition to being beautiful, she is lucky that she has come from the one career that makes a life in modeling look like one with longevity.

We are back at the École des Beaux-Arts, where my week started. This being an art school, the walls are wheat-pasted with broadsides that read, "Don't shit on yourselves any longer, shit on others!" and "The young make love, the old only make obscene gestures!"

The girls are dressed and undressed in under three minutes by pit-stop crews of attendants. Repairs are sewn directly onto their bodies. Between costumes, the models stand in high heels and thongs, topless. Surely this is some man's fantasy, I think. Sadly not my own, although a cocktail dress made entirely out of dyed-pink rabbit fur comes close.

There is only one more show to go. Viktor and Rolf, a forward-thinking Dutch duo, have chosen as their venue Trocadéro, the almost fascistically spare complex of buildings overlooking the Eiffel Tower. The interior is blessedly cool and full of fog lapping along the floor. We are instructed to descend to the basement hall quietly and slowly. We comply, since with roughly eight feet of visibility we are concentrating on not falling down the stairs. I find my seat and watch as a woman emerges from the mist. She still insists on wearing her sunglasses and talking on her cell phone, while holding her seat assignment three inches from her face. She is swallowed up in another cloud and I wonder how she will perform all these tasks with such limited sensory capacities. I listen for the sound of crashing chairs or the roar of the sea serpents who will devour her when she falls off the edge of the earth.

The show is all stark conceptualism. The writer and futurist guru Douglas Coupland has written the catalog's introductory essay and also came up with the names of each of the collection's twelve dresses. Titles like "MP3/NHK/'Daisy'/

Enter your 4-digit PIN number and press 'OK'/Mp3/Nihon Hoso Kyokai TV" and "OPD/PFD/'Hawk'/System error/ Please restart/Officially Pronounced Dead/PhotoShop File Document."

The show's beginning is announced by two gongs. There is no music, but that's no matter because the dresses themselves tintinnabulate with the garlands of brass bells that adorn them. The models jingle like Lapland reindeer, which is the only indication we have of their approach. The other sound is the steady stream of cursing coming from the frustrated photographers who are unable to get a clear shot.

How on earth would any of the Ladies get one of these garments through the metal detectors at the airport? But the larger question is an economic one. How does any of this sustain a business? I've been told that couture builds the prestige and identity of a house, it is the thing that moves the blue jeans and the sportswear and the fragrance, but Viktor and Rolf don't have a perfume to the best of my knowledge. How are they paying the craftspeople who are sewing these bells on? The wages for the final dress alone, the show's putative bridal gown—"KGB/LAX/'Rabbit'/Be Kind • Rewind/ Kommitet Gozudvastenoi Beznopasnosti/Los Angeles International Airport"—must have been fairly steep. It is entirely covered in bells, tipping the scale at close to a hundred pounds, I am sure. We can tell before we see it because it sounds like a chain gang of Jacob Marleys coming to get us. Out of the mist she comes, Carmen Kass, she of the perfect fuck-you strut. Her wings have finally been clipped. Even she can barely walk under the weight, plodding with the pained and rapturous vacancy of a medieval saint. A perfect coda to the week, this Slave of Fashion, bidding me good-bye. She shambles past and is obscured by another bank of clouds, leaving behind only the sound of her utmost vanquishment, her robes clanking like a martyr's chains.

BEAT ME, DADDY

What is it about house music that makes gay men want to buy underpants? The regular *whump, whump* from the street-level sound system of the Universal Gear store pulses up through the floor of the Washington headquarters of the Log Cabin Republicans, the largest gay and lesbian organization in the GOP.

As someone who can still barely comprehend the concept of Jewish conservatives, despite their shaming and undeniable existence, I know I am a naïve throwback to a time when both visible and invisible minorities largely allied themselves with progressive politics. Having only just arrived in D.C. on an overcast day in October 2003 for my first direct encounter with gay Republicans, I am a veritable Darwin in the Galápagos, slack-jawed in the presence of this confounding genus, a creature that seems to invite its own devouring; the cow helpfully outlining its tastiest cuts on its side with chalk, while happily pouring the A-1 sauce over its own head.

Mark Mead, director of public affairs, is familiar with my particular brand of astonishment. "I've heard it all. Everything from 'You guys are like Jewish Nazis' to 'What are you, the syrup lobby?' " What the Log Cabin Republicans really are, he informs me, is a band of political renegades, ten thousand strong. "We're the cutting edge of the gay civil rights movement."

I almost respond with a hearty "And I am Marie of Romania!" until I see that he is not joking.

Mead and I are sitting in his office, located on the second floor of a low brick building on Seventeenth Street near Dupont Circle, D.C.'s gay neighborhood. Out of keeping with the area, certainly worlds away from downstairs' Ecstasy-fueled dance-club soundtrack, this suite is among the least homosexual places I have ever been. With its mismatched laminate furniture, patterned industrial-strength nylon carpet, overhead fluorescent lighting, and scattered computer terminals, it could pass for any middling place of business: a paper supplier, an insurance broker. The walls are largely bare, save for a photo of super-butch, mustachioed Teddy Roosevelt, the ultimate Village People cop, along with a framed copy of the Gettysburg Address, a document absolutely central to the mythology of the Log Cabinites. Their name stems from the rough-hewn structure in which Honest Abe was born. The group's very identity as Republicans depends at least in part upon the belief that the party of Lincoln is at heart still, well, the party of Lincoln; an inclusive party, the Big Tent party. "Big Tent" is invoked in almost every conversation I have, a mantra about as descriptively apt as the wishful four-year-old at Halloween who announces "I'm a scary monster!" to every grown-up proffering candy.

I have arrived during strange and accelerated days for those toiling in gay rights. The Supreme Court overturned Texas's long-standing ban on sodomy in June 2003, and over the course of a few short months, the debate has graduated from the right to engage in private consensual sex to an open, although not necessarily civil, discussion of the freedom for gays and lesbians to marry. If anyone can be credited with firing the first shot in the battle, it would have to be justice Antonin Scalia, whose minority dissent darkly augured that the June decision could spell the end of all morals-based legislation in this country. The republic had been forcibly bound into a pair of buttered skis and was perched at the top of a slippery slope, at the bottom of which lay a land overrun by gay and lesbian weddings. An initiative called Marriage Protection Week concluded just prior to my arrival in town. Spearheaded by a loose coalition of far-right organizations, it consisted of little more than an official proclamation—signed by George W. Bush—which stated unequivocally in its third sentence that "Marriage is a union between a man and a woman." That can't have made gay Republicans feel terribly well liked under the Big Tent.

"I'm not in politics to be liked, I'm in politics to make change," says Mead.

A Mississippi native, Mead is a clean-cut, boyish man of forty-two, with a broad face and a ready smile, projecting suburban Dad stability, and a kind of "Kiss the Cook"–barbecue-apron-wearing good humor. He worked for a long time with Equality Georgia, a gay rights organization that lobbied for, and helped secure, domestic partnership benefits at large Georgia corporations like Coca-Cola. His best friend is a liberal Democrat who works for County Welfare in Los Angeles, although he admits they don't really talk politics. Despite his assertions to the contrary, he is a very likable guy, except for an odd moment in the first hour of our meeting, when he tells me about his life partner, who works at the EPA. The confirmation of the new head of the agency was being held up at that very moment by, among others, junior senator from New York Hillary Clinton, who was taking exception to the agency's obfuscation of the environmental dangers posed to rescue and salvage workers by the air at Ground Zero. Mead echoes the administration's party line to me. "*Everyone* knew the air was bad. They had respirators, but you know, cops and firemen can be real macho cowboys, 'We don't need respirators . . .'" he says. *Oh right*, I think, suddenly brought back to reality. *You're a Republican.*

Mead works in concert with Log Cabin's executive director, a man named Patrick Guerriero. Guerriero is thirty-six years old, a good-looking, swarthy, supersmart man. When we first meet, he has only been in Washington for ten months and is not yet a victim of that town's widespread disease, the scourge that obliterates the personal style of all who move there. There is still some smolder beneath the broadcloth. Elected to the Massachusetts House of Representatives at age twenty-five, he left in his third term to serve as the mayor of Melrose, the Boston suburb of thirty thousand where he grew up. He was reelected with more than eighty percent of the vote but stepped down to become the deputy chief of staff for then-governor of Massachusetts Jane Swift. She tapped him as her running mate for the following election. Guerriero would have been the nation's first openly gay lieutenant governor, but Swift withdrew from the race. He took over at Log Cabin in January of 2003.

We go to lunch together at a nearby Mexican restaurant. The only two people in the place on this gray day, we sit underneath strings of chili-pepper lights. It makes for a very sad fiesta. Perhaps abjection is just in the air as I can't help wondering why someone would take a blowtorch to such a promising political résumé. With the exception of that Jai Rodriguez fellow—the Culture expert on *Queer Eye for the Straight Guy*—Patrick Guerriero might just have the worst gay job in America.

"I had to wrestle with myself for three months before taking it," Guerriero says. In a nation divided almost equally between Democrat and Republican, he sees the Log Cabin presence in the party as a duty, unpleasant though it may be at times. Any significant legislation that is drafted and passed in this country requires bipartisan support, he says. "No one has ever given me the model to change America without doing what we're doing as a part of it. You can't get there by completely abandoning one American political party, you just can't. How do I keep my personal integrity and remain Republican? I wonder about that at least once a day, and I check my gut, and the response to my gut check is: 'You need to stay and fight this battle. If you leave, who's going to do it?' "

Who indeed? The amount of snickering and downright hostility that must go on behind his back among his supposed allies beggars the imagination. I remember a grim old joke about bigotry. "What's the definition of a kike?" I ask him. "A Jewish gentleman who has just left the room."

"I'm sure that happens. But I also bet when I leave the room on a number of occasions, the interaction of debate and dialogue will have changed some minds and some attitudes."

Minds and attitudes that he necessarily must change if Log Cabin is to be anything but a miserable failure within the party. Guerriero sees the debate over gay marriage as the right's last chance to ratify bigoted legislation before the juggernaut of history grinds them beneath its wheels, and the bigots will not give up without a fight. "The next phase is going to be ugly," he warns, "but they cannot beat the unstoppable force."

Unstoppable force! Ha! And I am Marie of . . . Oh.

It shouldn't be a surprise that Guerriero is willing to content himself with short shrift, given his other lifelong affiliations. "I have a lot of strikes against me," he jokes. "I'm a Catholic from the archdiocese of Boston, from a Democratic family, and I'm a Red Sox fan. I've chosen to stay in institutions I care about."

I suspect that Guerriero's family loves him no matter what his party affiliation, and last I checked the Red Sox didn't try to reverse the Curse of the Bambino by crowding all the homos into the obstructed-view seats. As for the archdiocese of Boston . . . 'nuff said. It's all well and good to stay in the institutions you care about, but wouldn't it be nice to feel that the institution, in turn, cared about you, or at least wasn't hell-bent on your eradication or, failing that, the legislating away of your rights? It seems a misdirected penance, this martyring oneself to a cause when the cause itself is the source of the suffering. Lovingly polishing the handle of the knife sticking into your side instead of just pulling it out. Surely, I suggest, there is a point at which one's self-respect has to count for something?

"You are counseling what the far right wants to happen," he says.

So why not give the far right its wish, I think? Why not work toward its effective and long-ranging disempowerment from someplace else? I must be wearing my bewildered *"What* the *fuck?"* look again, because Guerriero adds, "I know exactly what you're going through."

But I'm not the one going through it. It is Guerriero who has used the word "bearable" numerous times over the course of our lunch, always to justify his remaining in the job. My delusions are of a different, somewhat patronizing variety. Looking across the table, I keep thinking that Guerriero will take off the mask at any moment. Here we are, after all, away from the dreary office, both gay, enjoying a sprightly conversation about politics without rancor or name-calling. At some point, he will see the futility of trying to fight for gay rights within the Republican Party and off we'll go to the nearest independent bookstore (with a brief stop at the Phillips Collection to see its wonderful Edward Hoppers) to buy Al Franken's latest tome, all the while laughingly shaking our heads at Guerriero's misguided, delusional episode working for Satan. What I am feeling about Guerriero has been felt about intelligent, handsome, confirmed bachelors such as him from time immemorial. I am thinking: *I can change him.*

AS WE EMERGE from Log Cabin HQ onto Seventeenth Street that evening, Guerriero briefly locks eyes with a young man. They hold each other's gaze for a second or two, the universal gay semaphore for mutual attraction. "Boys," he sighs. "I never know if they're cruising me or glaring because they see me coming out of this office." I have come to pick up Mead and Guerriero, who are taking me to the inaugural reception for an advocacy group called Freedom to Marry.

The gathering is being held in a private home, a modern box of brick and glass on a tree-lined street of older brownstones. The place is a crush of people, mostly men still wearing their work clothes. I don't spend a lot of my waking life feeling terribly sexy, but in our nation's capital, I feel almost Genet-like by comparison. Spying openly gay, liberal Democrat Massachusetts congressman Barney Frank by the buffet table, I rush

over to try out on him—as a kind of rhetorical exercise—
Guerriero's theory that in this evenly divided nation, the future of gay rights is dependent on this band of rebels bravely
working for compromise on the right. He looks at me through
lowered eyes, as if to ask, *And how long have you been smoking crack?*

"They've been telling me 'We're just starting out' for fifteen
years," he says. "And they just don't deliver. One of the biggest
differences between the parties is on gay and lesbian issues."

"Say nice things about us, Barney," says Guerriero as he
passes through the crowd at that moment.

"No, Patrick. I've got to tell the truth." He turns back to
me. "They're woefully unsuccessful, but *he*," meaning Guerriero, "is intellectually honest, at least. Look, the argument
that this is better for gay rights makes no sense. They say,
'Well, isn't it good that we try to persuade the Republicans to
do better?' They helped put this administration in power. If it
was inevitable, then you can get credit for moderating its effects. But if you start the fire, you don't get any credit for putting it out. They're Republican for economic reasons," he
concludes.

The counterargument from gay Republicans to such a
charge is that while they may be (deeply, *deeply*) enamored of
Republican tax cuts, they are Republican for many reasons beyond mere economics. They are equally concerned with matters of national security, foreign policy, gun control, and
terrorism. They are not single-issue voters, not even around
their own sexual orientation. If Bush needs to gin up his base

with some homophobic saber-rattling by voicing support for a constitutional amendment banning gay marriage forever and always, so be it.

Such abject masochism may make for great Billie Holiday songs—it kind of ain't nobody's business if Lady Day is beat up by her papa; he isn't hoping to pack the courts with anti-choice troglodytes or to defund social security—but the Log Cabin blues have ramifications beyond the merely personal. It might be a price they are willing to pay for the sweet lovin' they feel they're getting from the rest of the GOP package, but I didn't sign on to get knocked around by someone else's abusive boyfriend.

In an article in *The New York Times,* a Log Cabin member, in excusing one of the President's gay-baiting screeds, dismissed it with "[it's] more for the constituents back home . . . just, you know, politics."

Those constituents back home to whom this fresh gay meat is routinely thrown, can't you just see them? A ragtag group of neglected souls who just need some empty, you know, politics to mollify them now and then. There are only about, you know, thirty million of them. Poor disenfranchised things. If only they had a cable news network of their own, or a ubiquitous, voluble punditocracy of intolerant gasbags catering to their worldview. Miraculously, though, they agree with Barney Frank about one thing: "Follow the money" is also their explanation for the existence of the Log Cabin Republicans.

"Anybody can be conservative on fiscal issues," says Robert

Knight, director of the conservative advocacy group the Culture and Family Institute, which sits squarely in the base of voters routinely courted with homophobic bouquets. "They're a Trojan horse within the GOP, carrying the left's message wrapped up in Republican garb. When it comes down to protecting the core of life, which is the family, they're on the other side." CFI is an affiliate organization of Concerned Women for America, which claims to be the largest public-policy women's group in the country. The Concerned Women are at the forefront of anti–gay marriage efforts along with other far right groups like the Family Research Council and the Traditional Values Coalition, the latter whose website even has a Homosexual Urban Legends page. Homosexual Urban Legends are not apocryphal tales of gay alligators in the sewers, gay pet Chihuahuas that turn out to actually be huge gay rats, or the woman who microwaved her gay cat, but are instead a refutation of the pseudo-science, sham statistics, and downright lies that are the evil tools of the Homosexual Agenda. The page has articles like "EXPOSED: 30% of teen suicide victims are homosexuals . . . NOT!!" and "Do Homosexuals Really Want the Right to Marry?" Apparently not. Marriage is just the innocuous tip of our lethal gay iceberg. The true gay objective is to use the right to marry as a stepping-stone to "destroying the concept of marriage altogether—and of introducing polygamy and polyamory (group sex) as 'families.'"

I have called Robert Knight to see what, if any, common ground exists between his group and its gay and lesbian con-

servative compatriots. Knight spent ten years at the Family
Research Council and was a senior fellow at the conservative
Heritage Foundation prior to that. He was also at the *Los
Angeles Times* and claims to have been a McGovern-voting
progressive. "I was a pretty radical guy. But I found out more
and more often that my liberal friends were covering up facts
in order to make their case."

He is nothing if not a man of strong convictions (something
I have always found attractive). I barely pronounce the Log
Cabin name at the beginning of our conversation when he
says, "Let me give you a quote here." He slows down his de-
livery. "The Log Cabin agenda to promote homosexuality is ut-
terly at odds with the GOP's self-styled image as a pro-family,
pro-marriage party."

Knight is ready with rebuttals to anything I bring up,
whether it's the statement that, according to the latest studies,
homosexuality is probably more a matter of chromosomes
("junk science"), or that gay men are no more likely to be pe-
dophiles than straight men ("There is a higher preponderance
of interest in sex with youth, as evidenced by the constant
themes in gay publications: boys boys boys").

Typically, Knight uses the word *homosexual* rather than *gay*,
all the better to emphasize that this is not an identity but
an illness, a reversible pathological behavior. Yet Knight's em-
phasis isn't so much on the behavior itself as on its host of
negative results: depression, rampant intravenous drug use
("It's well documented"), and ravaged, incontinent sphincters
("Older gays, y'know, have to wear diapers, because they've ru-

ined the rectum"). All of these are the wages of the homosexual's lifelong devotion to that one defining, until recently criminalized sexual act: sodomy. "Sodomy is their rallying cry," he says.

Well, it sure is *someone's* rallying cry. A lot of our hour-long conversation is taken up with talking about anal sex. I have never spoken so much about anal sex in my life.

"The anus is not a receptable, okay?" Knight says. "Using it as an entrance instead of an exit ramp is one of the most unhealthy things you can do with your body, and yet we're pretending that this is some sort of an identity. Like you're born with a need to put your penis down a guy's butt." He lets out a snort of incredulous *is-it-just-me-or-are-we-living-in-opposite-worlds?* laughter.

But if Knight displays an obsession with the mechanics of sodomy—simultaneously mesmerized and sickened by the tumescent, pistoning images of it that must loop through his head on a near-constant basis—he is notably impervious to an image he conjures when I submit as how HIV is transmissible through normative, upstanding, God-sanctioned heterosexual congress as well.

"Not as easily," he says. "The vagina is designed to accommodate a penis. It can take a lot of punishment."

My regards to Mrs. Knight.

IN HIS VIEW, failing enrollment in one of the faith-based ex-gay "recovery" programs, there is little hope for the homosexual and absolutely no quarter for them in the party. Even the civil benefits of partnership—hospital visitation, inheritance rights, social security—would be tantamount to granting special treatment in his eyes. "If you operate on the fringes of society, you can expect a little inconvenience."

Knight doesn't hate homosexuals, he assures me; he even has gay friends (*there's* a dinner party I'd like to see). He would feel pity for us if we were simply benighted sinners, hermetically contained within our own diseased communities. But we aren't, and this has him scared. Knight's terrified vision is of *The Protocols of the Elders of Sodom* variety. Like those Nazi-era newspaper cartoons of hook-nosed Jewish bankers in waistcoats and silk top hats fondling bags of money or greedily clutching the globe itself, Knight sees a monolithic shadow empire of homosexuals. An insinuating, pernicious threat, hell-bent on dismantling that most holy, delicate, and imperiled institution: the American Family. He will not, *cannot,* stand idly by and allow this to happen.

"You have to understand that the greatest threat to American freedom today from within is the gay rights movement. It has the potential to criminalize Christianity and to single people out for persecution if they don't go along with whatever the gay rights folks want. The Boy Scouts serve as a prime example of that: 'Disagree with us, we'll cut your throats.'"

"NO ONE BECOMES a Log Cabin Republican because they assume it's going to be easy," says Guerriero, when I tell him about my interview with Vaginal Punisher Robert Knight. Life

under the Big Tent means having to countenance such viru-
lent hatred against one, I guess. I watch *Fighting for Freedom,*
an hour-long compilation of Log Cabin television clips in
which Guerriero goes up against detractor after detractor. He
is well-spoken and composed throughout. Holding his own
against congresswoman Marilyn Musgrave, one of the framers
of the constitutional amendment, he suggests that she "seek
counseling if a gay or lesbian in North America somehow
threatens your marriage." But when it comes to what so infuriates Barney Frank, namely making the support of the LCR
contingent upon . . . *anything,* really, he exhibits a maddening
propensity toward blind devotion. Sensing this, Ann Curry, on
the *Today* show, asks him point-blank, "Does the President actually even risk the gay Republican vote?" His response is,
"Unlike other organizations, Log Cabin Republicans are loyal.
We don't expect to get our way all of the time." On CNN with
(the absolutely divine) Anderson Cooper, Mark Mead is pit-
ted against Ken Connor of the Family Research Council.
Connor plainly states that if the President alienates the pro-
family base, he does so at his own peril. "The final analysis
will have a chilling effect. Subtraction of many more numbers
than the gay-lesbian vote." Cooper then turns to Mead who,
even after this demonstration of how it is done, puts forth a
cheerful and toothless, "James Carville wrote a book on political loyalty called *Stickin'.* The Log Cabin Republicans are
gonna *stick* with George Bush. He may not be able to count
on Ken and some other folks, but he can count on the Log
Cabin Republicans."

I yell at my VCR, "Schmuck! Don't tell the President that!" Stating on national television that the President can use you as electoral cannon fodder and still get your vote seems as effective a piece of rhetoric as picketing a restaurant with signs that read THE BOSS IS A REAL ASSHOLE AND THERE ARE MAGGOTS IN THE CHICKEN SALAD. WE EAT HERE EVERY DAY.

Then I calm down. I think, *This must be part of some canny strategy.*

Right?

OVER THE MANY months that I talk with and keep tabs on Guerriero, I am visited by a recurring image of him as a frog in a cauldron, surrounded by baby carrots and oyster crackers, splashing around in the gradually boiling water, unmindful of the fact that he is slowly becoming soup.

On February 24, 2004, when George Bush unequivocally calls for the constitutional amendment, I think Guerriero might finally be induced to jump out of the pot. What more needs to happen? Those seeking the Democratic nomination have also refused to go on record in support of gay marriage, so the President's remarks seem only to serve as a decisive fuck you to Patrick and his kind. When I call Guerriero up, he doesn't even bother with hello.

"Want my job, David?" he jokes.

"I don't," I reply. "Do *you* want your job?"

I expect him to say, *No, I don't want my job, they've gone too far this time.*

Instead, his answer is a simple and immediate "Of course."

His mission remains clear. "Some folks need to stand on the front lines of the Republican Party," he says, "and that's us."

I needn't bother pointing out that the gunfire is actually coming from behind him. He does at least admit that this is "probably a new chapter for our organization, but we're ready for it."

Does that new chapter include withholding their endorsement of Bush for reelection? It is too early to say.

Guerriero is right about one of the very first things he told me: progress is inevitable, although things may well get a good deal uglier before they improve. Perhaps not immediately, but in a few years, the news footage of those who so vehemently oppose gay rights today will resemble the grainy images of the racists who turned the firehoses on marchers in Alabama. Why on earth, then, would one choose to take one's place in history by throwing one's lot in with the modern-day equivalents of Bull Connor? *See there? The person in the background opening up the hydrant? That's me!*

I finally come clean about a theory that has been percolating in the back of my mind since that first day in the Mexican restaurant more than six months ago. I tell him, "I keep thinking to myself, 'Patrick is so smart and so articulate and seems genuinely socially engaged. Ten years from now, I bet he's going to be a Democrat.'"

He takes no offense at this. "You and I don't come to the same conclusion. Ten years from now, I hope people will be able to look back and say, 'You know what? A small band of pretty courageous, conservative gay and lesbian Americans stood up to their party. It wasn't easy, they were criticized, they made some mistakes, there were days when it was difficult to understand what they were doing.' I think we have an obligation as Republicans to be on the front lines of this, even if we're taken down in the process, it's worth it."

We have that conversation early in 2004, when thoughts of being "taken down in the process" are still quaintly theoretical. The hope is that the evangelical base will have been sufficiently mollified by the President's periodic support for the amendment that by the time of the convention, the issue will have been successfully disappeared. But the prime-time presence of mediagenically moderate Republicans like Giuliani and Schwarzenegger on the convention stage cannot soften the fact that when the official GOP platform is released, it comes out unequivocally against not just gay marriage but civil unions as well.

On September 8, 2004, one week after the Republicans have decamped from New York, the Log Cabin Republicans officially withhold their endorsement of George Bush for president. Instead, they will shift their "financial and political resources to defeating the radical right and supporting inclusive Republican candidates for the U.S. Senate and House of Representatives."

ANTI—GAY MARRIAGE AMENDMENTS that are on the ballots in eleven critical swing states all pass with wide, decisive margins of support. Some postelection wisdom is that it is these measures specifically that really got out the vote, galvanizing people and resulting in unprecedented turnout among those most desperate to tie the flaps of the Big Tent securely shut. The Log Cabin slogan of "Inclusion Wins"—an appeal to fellow Republicans' better natures, and a reminder of the divisive culture war that is thought to have contributed to the defeat of Bush's father in 1992—seems hopelessly out of touch. To be perfectly schoolyard about it, if the exit polls are any indication, inclusion is for fags.

A week after the election, Guerriero issues a statement. "We lost," he states plainly. "If we listen to those attempting to sanitize or sugarcoat the post-election analysis, we are doomed to repeat our mistakes and destined for more setbacks in the years ahead."

He lays out a plan for regrouping and completely restrategizing their struggle. The community needs to focus on the heartland and not just the coasts. "Like it or not, Michael Moore, Bruce Springsteen, and Rosie O'Donnell will never convince the Iowa farmer, the South Carolina veteran, or the West Virginia coal miner to be on our side. Much more important than increasing attendance at all of our organizations' expensive black-tie dinners is the work we should be doing hosting rural barbecues and town hall meetings for honest discussions with people who disagree with us." But the LCR should also not shy away from going on the offensive. With the marriage protection ballot measures passed and the institution fully protected as a sacrosanct pact between one man and one woman, it is time to expose the radical right's true agenda, which is the stripping away of all gay civil rights.

Reading along, Guerriero's statement seems well written, reasonable, and eloquent, and I find much to admire and agree with, like, "it should never be easier to get 5,000 people to a circuit party than it is to get 500 people to pick up the phone and call their Congressman." He goes on to analyze the various doomed strategies and self-sabotage that lethally mired the LCR. One was in choosing their friends poorly. "While we need to continue developing progressive allies for our fight, we should be cautious about taking on all of their baggage at the same time. The gay wedge issue was effective in this election because our opponents were successful at clumping our struggle for equality in with anti-war protesters, the Janet Jackson wardrobe malfunction, the move to take God out of the Pledge, the late-term abortion debate, and a whole range of other cultural issues. We need to talk less about all the rights we want and do not have. Instead, we need to talk more about the moral and ethical responsibilities we are ready to accept as our life-long relationships are recognized."

The Log Cabin hope is that by being law-abiding, well-mannered, income-generating, monogamous Hathaway-shirt men—oozing nothing more threatening or boat-rocking than wholesome, heteronormative presentability—they will finally be granted entry into the tent. If they were shut out in 2004, it was because they were seen to be bellyaching about a host of other causes that had nothing to do with them or their struggle.

And there it is, in a heartbreaking little nutshell, the thing that has been bothering me and that I have been trying to articulate for more than a year. Not to get too Henry Fonda in his final monologue in *The Grapes of Wrath* about it, but wherever there is a woman whose health is endangered because the right has outlawed a medical procedure, Guerriero and the Log Cabinites will be there. Whenever the puritanical hypocrisy of the FCC gives violence (and Rupert Murdoch) a free pass, while selectively demonizing sex, they'll be there. And when the right continues to try to efface the separation between church and state, why, they'll be there, too. Whether they like it or not. The connection between all these issues and gay rights is glaringly direct. If I can see it, why can't Guerriero? What accounts for this myopia?

Guerriero once said to me that no one becomes a gay Republican because they think it's going to be easy. Unfortunately, I'm more inclined to agree with both Barney Frank and Robert Knight. Greed trumps principle as people vie for passage on the Bush administration representation-without-taxation gravy train. Those sacred GOP tenets of smaller government, personal responsibility, and fiscal conservatism are all code for "easy." Or at least easier. It's a cargo-cult fantasy of a Karl Rovian utopia where the social safety net has been dismantled and the economic windfall rains down upon the lucky few. Come for the cash, stay for the homophobia.

There will likely never be a shared trip to the Phillips

Collection for Patrick Guerriero and myself. I doubt he'd much want to hang out with me, either, but I cannot help feeling about him what has been felt about intelligent, handsome, confirmed bachelors such as him from time immemorial. I think: *What a waste.*

WHATSIZFACE

I am not a handsome man. All that means is that my face has never been my fortune. Luckily for me, it hasn't been my punch line, either. I have some pretty eyes and, like everyone, I have my moments. I may even be thought attractive by those who love me, but that is emphatically not the same as the irrefutable mathematics of plane and placement that make for true beauty.

As a teenager reading *Death in Venice*, I understood the world to be divided between the Aschenbachs and the Tadzios. There are those who gaze, and those who are gazed upon. I am not talking about the natural inequity of attention that the old bestow upon the young—we are all hardwired to respond to babies, for example, but it would take the rare and deeply odd child to singsong to a grown-up, "Who's got a cute receding hairline? Oh yes it is." I am talking about within one's own cohort: some are destined to promenade the Lido in Venice, blooming like flowers under the heat of appreciative stares, while the rest of us are born to watch, sweating through our grimy collars and eating our musty strawberries while the plague rolls in.

Inveterate Aschenbach that I have always been, we are at peace, my face and I, although it can be a tenuous cease-fire. A certain degree of dissatisfaction with my features is part of my cultural birthright. In my largely Jewish high school scores of girls got new noses for their birthdays, replacing their fantastic Litvak schnozes with "the Mindy," as Paul Rudnick has dubbed that shiny-skinned, characterless lump. Despite the prevalence and remarkable timing of these operations, coinciding as they so often did with upcoming Sweet Sixteens, they were always framed as life-or-death necessities—emergency procedures to repair lethally deviated septa and restore imperiled breathing. Even then, we knew enough to lie. Elective cosmetic surgery was the province of the irretrievably shallow. It was also a largely female pursuit. For most boys, failing the unlikely scenario wherein you infiltrated the mob, turned state's evidence, and got a new set of features thanks to the good doctors at the witness protection program, your face was an irreducible fact.

Still, without benefit of a mirror I can easily reel off all of the things I might change, given the opportunity. Starting at the top, they include a permanent red spot on the left side of my forehead; a brow pleated by worry: a furrow between my eyebrows so deep that at times it could be a coin slot; purple hollows underneath my eyes that I've had since infancy, and, also since childhood, lines like surveyors marks on my cheeks—placeholders for the inevitable eye bags I will have; a nose more fleshy and wide than prototypically Semitic, graced with a bouquet of tiny gin blossoms resulting from years of using neither sunscreen nor moisturizer; a set of those Fred Flintstone nasal creases down to the corners of my mouth; a permanent acne scar on my right cheek; a planklike expanse of filtrum between the bottom of my nose and the top of my too-thin upper lip; and, in profile, a double chin.

None of which is really a problem in New York City. Being a little goofy looking suits the supposed literary life-of-the-mind I lead here. (What a paper-thin lie. There are days when I'd throw out every book I own for the chance to be beautiful just once. Reading is hard, to paraphrase that discontinued Barbie.) Seriously contemplating the erasure or repair of any of these is inconceivable within the city limits. It's too small a town. There is a place, though, where the sunny notion of physical perfection and its achievement by any means necessary is carried unashamedly on the smoggy, orange-scented air: swimming pools, movie stars. Cue the banjo music.

I MAKE CONSULTATIONS with two Beverly Hills surgeons. I want them to tell me what they might do, as though I had limitless inclination and resources, with no input from me. The reason for my silence is that I'd like outside confirmation of those things that are true flaws and those that are dysmorphic delusions on my part. There is also the vain hope that it is all dysmorphic delusion. That if I fail to bring it to their attention, somehow it will turn out that I've had the nose of a Greek statue all along. Primarily, though, I am hoping to catch them out in a moment of unchecked avarice; instead of proposing the unnecessary pinning back of my ears, I imagine them letting slip with their true purpose, as in, "I recommend the Italian ceramic backsplashes in my country house kitchen." Or "You'd look much better if my toxic punishing bitch of an ex-wife didn't insist on sending our eight-year-old daughter, Caitlin, to riding lessons in Malibu for $300 an hour."

GARTH FISHER'S PRACTICE is decorated with a grandeur disproportionate to the space, like a studio apartment tricked out with pieces from the set of *Intolerance*. The waiting area has overstuffed sofas, a small flat-screen TV in the corner, tasseled wall sconces, and a domed oculus in the low ceiling, painted with clouds. Fisher's office is full of bulky antique furniture in dark wood with turned legs, armoires, walnut bookcases. Behind his desk are many photographs of his wife, Brooke Burke, a model and television personality. Were I differently placed on the Kinsey scale, I might even pronounce her "hot," dropping my voice an octave and adding an extra syllable to the word. She is a near-perfect beauty.

Fisher himself is also nice-looking, a handsome man in his

early forties. Blue-eyed and chestnut-haired, he has a bit of the early-seventies Aqua Velva hunk about him. I ask him, looking directly at the enviable cleft in his chin, if he's had any work done himself. Very little. A tiny bit of botox between his brows and some veneers on his teeth. He also had his nose done, to correct some football injuries. To my dismay, he is similarly conservative in his approach to others. Of the eight potential patients he saw that day, he refused to take on seven of them. Some were not candidates while others had unreasonable expectations about what plastic surgery can realistically do, even now.

"This is the Dark Ages. This is like 1904," he says. Future generations will be amazed by the inevitable advances, he predicts. For now he is more than willing to allow other doctors to use their patient populations as the guinea pigs for new and experimental treatments. He has not done a penile augmentation, for example ("scary business"), neither does he offer those silicone pectoral or calf implants.

"I want a simple life. All I've got to do is do a good job and tell the truth."

The only reason he agrees to give me unsolicited advice is that he knows I am a writer (indeed, the only way I could get an appointment with two top Beverly Hills plastic surgeons is that they know I am a writer). He remains notably uncomfortable with the charade. "If someone comes in here like this," he pulls his ears out from his head like Dumbo, "and all they want fixed is the mole on their chin, then that's all I'm going to mention." Assured of my thick skin, he eventually allows as how he might "clean some things up" that steal focus from my eyes.

We go into an examining room where he keeps his computer simulator. The process begins with taking two photographs—the "befores." I look the way I always do, but it's embarrassing to see myself up on the monitor with another person sitting there. My profile looks careworn, simultaneously bald and hairy. My eyes are sunk into craters of liver-colored flesh, and my ear is a greasy nautilus, as if I'd just come from listening to a deep-fat fryer.

Fisher demonstrates his morphing tool by drawing a circle around my chin with the mouse. Pulling the cursor, he extends my jaw out like a croissant. It is a fabulous toy. I want to wrest the mouse from his control and really go to town, giving myself fleshy horns, pointy corkscrew ears. If he would only let me, I would pull out the flanges of my nostrils until they looked like the wings of Eero Saarinen's TWA terminal at JFK. "But your chin is perfect," he says, snapping it and me back to reality. "Three millimeters behind your bottom lip." Instead, he points out how the end of my nose droops down to the floor, while the arch of my nostrils is very high. (I write "too high" in my notebook before realizing that these are my words, not his.) He raises the tip, lowers my nostrils, and then straightens out the slope of the nose itself. It is subtle and aquiline. He then smoothes out the area under my eyes. In real life this would involve the removal of some fat and tightening up the skin. Finally, he points to the small vertical indentation between my brows, just like the one he had before botox. He recommends a small amount of the neurotoxin, just enough to smooth it out without robbing me of my capacity to emote. Of all the features that render me less than perfect, I've actually always sort of been attached to those that lend me an air of gravitas, covering up my shortcomings of character and intellect. I ask if it's all right to leave it as is. "Well," he shrugs, "it's okay if you're playing a lawyer or a judge." Instead, I get him to give me a slight Mick Jagger moue. "I don't like those lips, but I'll let you have them." He plumps up my mouth.

The photographs are printed out, the two images side by side against a dark background with no discernible seam between them. I am a set of twins. My original self seems a melancholic killjoy. His reengineered brother, on the other hand, looks clean and a little haughty. And how about that marvelous new nose! Pointy, sharp, a weapon. Despite that old stereotype about Jewish intellectual superiority, I think I appear cleverer as well ("perspicacious," as my ethnically cleansed self might say). Fisher's instinct about my new mouth was also right on the money. It gives me the beginnings of a snarl, like I've wedged a handful of Tic Tacs in front of my upper teeth.

But even my misbegotten new upper lip cannot dampen my spirits. I step out into the beautiful California dusk to catch a cab with a spring in my step. I'm feeling handsome, as though Fisher's changes were already manifest on my face and not just in the envelope of photographs I clutch. Reality soon sets in. The sidewalk of Santa Monica Boulevard simply ends without warning and I have to dart, terrified, across four lanes of traffic. I cannot find a taxi on the deserted leafy streets of Beverly Hills, and I have to walk all the way back to my hotel. "Good evening," the beautiful young doorman says to me when I arrive, an hour and a half later. He smiles in my direction, but his eyes are looking just above my left ear.

Studying the photographs the next morning, I am already experiencing some misgivings. It is not the regret of "What have I done?" that dogs me so much as a feeling that I want more. I briefly curse Garth Fisher's innate professionalism and hope that Richard Ellenbogen, my next surgeon, will not hang back and keep me from achieving my true physical glory.

If his office is any indication, I'm in luck. Where Fisher's was the McMansion version of the baths at Pompeii, Richard Ellenbogen's Sunset Boulevard practice (hard by the Hamburger Hamlet where Dean Martin ate every day) defies easy aesthetic description. It is an astonishment of styles and motifs. The reception desk is framed by two arching female figureheads as might be found on the prow of a Spanish galleon. The walls of the waiting room are peach plaster set with Tudor timbers. There is an ornamental brick fireplace in the corner, sofas in floral chintz, and everywhere, absolutely everywhere—on the mantel, along the plate rail (hung with swags of floral chintz bunting)—are ormolu clocks, Bakelite and old wooden radios, commemorative plates, lamps and small sculptures of those young, barely pubescent deco-era girls, the kind who festoon old movie-palace plaster and frequently hold aloft globe lights. All of it in under 150 square feet.

There is a benevolence to this crowded exuberance; one's own physical flaws shrink to nothing in the midst of such riotous excess. The staff is friendly and funny. "Here to get your breasts done?" cracks one woman when she sees me. Another confides, "Sometimes he," meaning Ellenbogen, "will just say to a patient, 'You don't need this. Buy a new dress and save your money.' We love our patients."

Ellenbogen is known for fat grafting and facial reshaping. Instead of pulling and tightening a face, he replaces the fat in the areas that used to be fuller, before aging and gravity did their work. For a patient in their mid-fifties, for example, he will analyze a photograph of them at half that age and isolate the facial regions in need of filling. The patients I look at in his albums do seem *juicy,* for lack of a better word, although the result looks not so much younger as vegetal. They look like Arcimboldo paintings, those Renaissance portraits constructed entirely out of fruit. To give them their due, they don't look like drum-tight gorgons, either. In folder after folder, I do not come across even one of those monstrous surgerized analogues of Joan Rivers. Where are those faces, I wonder aloud to Ellenbogen?

"We call that the New York look," he says. Apparently, there is less need for that kind of wholesale renovation in Los Angeles, where Hollywood hopefuls have been a self-selecting group for almost a century. "People are prettier here. It's now the children and grandchildren of Sandra Dee. In New York, you've still got all those great Jewish immigrant faces." Ellenbogen is allowed to say this, possessed of one as he is himself. (He's had some botox, his neck done, and lipo on his love handles, although he still supports a somewhat cantilevered belly as befits a man of sixty.)

He doesn't do computer imaging. "It's hokey. It's used by people who aren't artists. It's not a true representation of what a surgeon can actually do. It's like a real estate agent saying, 'This would be such an incredible view if you just planted some trees here and put in a garden . . .'" Instead, he takes two Polaroids and, using a small brush, mixes together unbleached titanium and burnt umber and paints the changes on one of them. Like Fisher, even with carte blanche, Ellenbogen only envisions minor treatments. Again with the straightening of the nose and raising the tip (one hour), he would also build out my chin a little bit, using a narrow curving strip of milky white silicone—like something from the toe of a high-end running shoe—fed down through the mouth behind the lower lip (ten minutes), and a final procedure (fifteen minutes) in which he would inject fat into my extremely deep nasojugal folds, those tear troughs under my eyes. (Garth Fisher is not a fan of regrafting. "You'd love your doctor for six months," and no longer, he implies.) Total cost, around $12,000.

There is nothing so intimately known as our own face. Even the most deprived existence provides opportunities to gaze into a reflective surface now and then—puddles of standing water, soup spoons, the sides of toasters. We know what pleases us, and also have a fairly good sense of what we would change if we could. Sometimes, though, we just get it plain wrong. Ellenbogen shows me a photo of a young man in his

twenties; a pale, strawberry blond with the kind of meek profile that gets shoved into lockers. "This kid came in and
wanted me to fix his nose. 'It's too big!' he said. I told him, 'It's
not your nose. I'll prove it to you. I'll build out your chin. If you
don't like it, I'll take it out and do your nose for free.'"
Ellenbogen was right. The merest moving forward of the jaw
has made the nose recede. The change is remarkable.

The fellow may have been focusing on the wrong feature,
but at least he wanted *something*. There is a reason that both
Fisher and Ellenbogen were so reluctant to suggest procedures to me. An unspecified and overarching desire for change
speaks to a dissatisfaction probably better served by a psychiatrist. One surgeon I spoke to will not treat people in their first
year of widowhood for just that reason. To briefly rant about
The Swan, the television show that takes depressed female
contestants—all of whom seem to need little more than to
change out of their sweat suits and get some therapy—and
makes them all over to look like the same trannie hooker: what
makes *The Swan* truly vile is that for the months that these
women are being carved up like so much processed poultry, all
of the mirrors in their lives are covered over. Such willing ab-
rogation of any say or agency in how they will be transformed
by definition means that in the real world, they would not be
candidates for surgery. It is the very sleaziest of all the plastic-
surgery makeover shows—quite a distinction, that; like being
voted the Osbourne child with the fewest interests.

Garth Fisher, in what might be considered an unconscious
act of penance for contributing to the culture in which something like *The Swan* can exist (he is the in-house surgeon for

the comparatively classier *Extreme Makeover*), has created a five-hour DVD series called *The Naked Truth About Plastic Surgery*. Each hour-long disk is devoted to a different procedure and region of the body—breast augmentation, brow lifts, etc.

In spirit, *The Naked Truth* is more educational tool than sales pitch. It is refreshingly up front about the complications that can arise, like bad scarring, hematoma, numbness, pigment irregularities, infection, skin loss, even embolism and death. In the liposuction section, there is a shot of Fisher in the operating room. The backs of the patient's legs are shiny brown from the pre-surgical iodine wash, and crisscrossed with felt-tip marker. Fisher is sawing away under the shuddering skin with the cannula, a tool resembling a sharp, narrow pennywhistle attached to a hose. There is a savagery to his movements, the way one might angrily go back and forth over a particularly tenacious piece of lint with a vacuum cleaner. He looks up at the camera, his arm going the whole time. Although wearing a mask, his eyes crinkle in an unmistakable "Well, hello there!" smile.

There are shots of clear plastic containers of extracted fat— frothy, orange-yellow foam floating atop a layer of dark blood—and pictures of postoperative faces looking like Marlon Brando after he's been worked over in *On the Waterfront*. Such footage might have once had a deterrent effect but is now familiar to any toddler who has ever been parked in front of The Learning Channel. That these images have to be followed up by the cautionary tone of a narrator who says, "just because something *can* be done does not mean it *should* be done" and "if you can reach your goal without surgery, then you are better off," speaks to how far down the rabbit hole we've tumbled. It's as if the whole country regularly watched newsreel footage of buses full of children going off of cliffs and was still blithely picking up the phone to make bookings with Greyhound.

I might be more apt to drink the Kool-Aid if I was more impressed by the results. The before and after photos of liposuction, for example, do show a reduction in volume. But if I were to endure the risks of general anesthetic, the pain, the constriction garment that must be worn like a sausage casing for weeks after the surgery, and the months-long wait for final results, I wouldn't just want a flatter stomach with no trace of love handles. I would insist upon the tortoiseshell reticulation of a six-pack, that abdominal Holy Grail. That's hard to achieve with liposuction. There is a procedure that replicates the look, called "etching," where the coveted tic-tac-toe pattern is suctioned out of the adipose tissue, giving the appearance of musculature with no muscles present; morphology absent of structure, like the false bones in McDonald's creepy McRib sandwich. Garth Fisher doesn't recommend or offer it. Gain weight, he points out, and the artificially differentiated lobes of your fat expand and rise from your stomach like a pan of buttermilk biscuits.

IN THE END, it is neither thrift nor fear of the knife that deters me. Far more than the physical transformation, it would be the very decision to go ahead with it that would render me unrecognizable to myself.

I once bleached my hair almost to platinum for a part in a short film. It lent me a certain Teutonic unapproachability, which I liked. But as it grew out, it faded to an acid, Marshmallow Peep yellow and my head started to look like a drugstore Easter-promotion window. Dark roots and straw-dry hair look fine on a college kid experimenting with peroxide, but I looked like a man of a certain age with a bad dye job clutching at his fleeting youth with bloody fingernails. I could see pity in the faces of strangers who passed me on the street. *Mutton dressed as lamb*, they were thinking. To all the world, I was the guy who broadcasts that heartbreaking and ambivalent directive: "Look at me, but for the reasons you used to!"

It must be murder to be an aging beauty, a former Tadzio, to see your future as an ignored spectator rushing up to meet you like the hard pavement. What a small sip of gall to be able to time with each passing year the ever-shorter interval in which someone's eyes focus upon you. And then shift away.

FASTER

It was turning out to be an anxious Christmas season. Too many were the early mornings spent sitting at the table, insomniac in the gray dawn, thinking to myself, *Eggs would be good*. Not for eating but for the viscous wrath of my ovo-barrage. It seemed only a matter of time before I was lobbing my edible artillery out the window at the army of malefactors who daily made my life such a buzzing carnival of annoyance. I could almost feel the satisfying, sloshy heft of my weapons as I imagined them leaving my hands and raining down upon my targets: the pair of schnauzers two doors down, with their loathsome, skittish dispositions, barking and yelping all day long; their owner, with her white hair styled like Marlene

Dietrich's in *Blonde Venus,* who allows them to pee freely on the garbage that some poor sanitation worker then has to pick up; the leather-clad schmuck immediately next door, a cigar-smoking casual life-ruiner with his mufflerless motorcycle. All would taste my All Natural, Vegetarian Feed, Grade A Extra Large brand of justice!

Clearly, actions would have to be taken. Such short-fused intervals are an occasional and inevitable by-product of city life, but they are usually the kind of private ravings best kept to oneself. When fractured logic threatens to make the leap from fantasy to reality, and from dairy case to gun show, the center is not holding. I have never been a poster boy for serenity, but I knew I needed to restore some semblance of inner peace. In search of a fix much quicker than my weekly forays into the talking cure, I came upon an ancient and proven practice, one that exists in every culture and religious tradition as a means to attaining calm and an alternate plane of consciousness: an extended fast. Buddha did it, Jesus did it, even Pythagoras and George Bernard Shaw did it. It's like a Cole Porter song from the world's least-fun musical. Can the gulf that exists between me and a placid equanimity really be bridged just by not eating for a little while? I would find out, or possibly die trying.

I found my program on the Web. This sounds more irresponsible than it really is. All of the fasts I researched follow much the same model and promise much the same results. I simply chose the place that looked most legitimate, that has been around the longest and had the most traceable address.

As a first-timer, I opted for the shortest one offered, twenty days. Actually, "twenty days" is a bit of a misnomer, it's really only two weeks of eating truly nothing, with three transitioning days of restricted eating on either end. For about $300, I am provided with an exhaustive regimen that includes the recipe for a special broth I have to drink that will provide me with much-needed potassium and electrolytes so that I don't keel over like Karen Carpenter, a schedule of when I am to drink it, along with the times for the juices and herbal teas that will make up the rest of my diet, as well as a plan for healthy eating for the remainder of my life post-fast. It's like a correspondence spa. Guiding me is the center's founder and president, a man I will call Brian. Based in California, he will respond almost immediately to the questions I send him by e-mail.

It briefly crosses my mind to start before the holiday parties are done with, as an added test of my ascetic resolve. I have visions of myself standing in crowded rooms, my hands folded modestly in front of me, my friends draining their glasses of Yuletide hooch while I quietly and beatifically turn away one cute waiter after another. In the end, I realize that such public and grandiose abstemiousness would miss the point of the whole enterprise. I go through the season swilling back liquor, scarfing down canapés, and vainly making eyes at the catering staff, exhausting myself and feeling crapulent, ready to begin in early January. The clean, white muslin of a new year.

The transition in—three days of two meals per day, one of raw fruit and one of raw vegetables—is easy and pleasurable.

I drop a pound each day. I walk uptown from my apartment one morning, taking in bracing lungfuls of icy air. The spire of the Chrysler Building glitters in the distance, the bare limbs of the winter trees in Gramercy Park glow ochre against the cloudless blue sky. My head sings with clarity. *I can do this,* I think excitedly.

Forty-eight hours later, Day One of the fast proper, I rise and begin what will be my new daily ritual for the next two weeks. My mornings start with the showstopper: an enema of warm water, chamomile tea, and eight drops of lemon juice. This ritual will soon become a necessity when, after a few days of taking in no food, my brain's evacuation impulse will shut down. I will have to help my body along. I am to hold it in for fifteen minutes, lying on a towel on the bathroom floor. This is followed by a dry skin rubbing with a natural bristle brush (circular movements beginning at the extremities and progressing in toward my heart), a shower (switching to luke-warm/cool for the rinse to close my pores and prevent colds), and breakfast of eight to twelve ounces of broth. At other points during the day—I cannot say exactly when because this is proprietary, copyrighted information—I will consume fruit juice, vegetable juice, herbal tea, and, finally, more broth just before bed. All liquid must be of a waterlike consistency. Apparently even the merest trace of pulp or puree would be enough to kick my brain's appestat mechanism back into gear, making me hungry. I buy a fine-mesh strainer and filter my broth with the concentration and devotion of a Trappist monk.

By 11:00 a.m. on the first day, I already feel like a dog's

breakfast; light-headed and lousy. Not hungry by any means, but sleepy and in the vise grip of a headache. Even conversation is taxing. I become hyperaware of the effortful deflation of my lungs that speech requires. My breath gives out by the end of my sentences. It's easily endurable for now, with my raft still in view of the shore, but what about the third day, or the ninth, I think? I get scared wondering how I will manage, even though I have been told repeatedly that it all changes by Day Four—hunger dissipates, energy increases, and the true brilliance of the experience begins to manifest. The prospect of what I might find has me quite excited, in those moments when I can focus on it, but right now, I cannot fathom two weeks of this. It all seems unattainably theoretical.

To better understand the physiology of what I'm feeling, I speak to Lisa Sanders, a doctor at Yale who spent five years analyzing the science behind more than seven hundred different diets. Apparently my sluggishness has everything to do with the sudden drop-off in my consumption of carbohydrates. With no incoming fuel in the form of food, my body is beginning to make the switch to consuming its own fat sources, known as ketones. The shift is not automatic. It takes place over the course of a few days. Until then, I will feel tired and out of sorts, but once the ketones kick in, Sanders says, people report returning to feeling quite normal. Even better than normal. According to what I've been reading, I expect I will feel downright marvelous. I ask Sanders why that might be.

"Ketones reduce your appetite, and they are your brain's preferred fuel. Maybe something about that makes you feel good," she says.

My fasting-center reading materials explain the feeling shitty and subsequent elevation in mood quite differently. Ketones, carbohydrates, and switching fuel sources never come up. It is all about toxins. As an urban North American living in the twenty-first century, with a fairly omnivorous diet—including the occasional dreaded hamburger—I have a surpassingly toxic body, with an average of five to ten pounds of toxins housed in my cells. My nerves and organs are so coated with this ubiquitous, sludgy film of judgment-clouding, character-distorting poison that I am living a less-than-optimal life. Chemical fertilizers, pesticides, old vaccinations and X-rays, remnants of medication, heavy metals, artificial colorings, flavorings, sweeteners, preservatives all conspire to make me less than the best David I can be. Apparently the reason I feel so rotten for the first few days of my fast is that the poisons are leaving the relatively inert resting places they have carved out in my cells and are passing through my skin and, most important, my colon, once more exerting their noxious effects. Stuff that hurts going in will hurt coming out, I am told.

And it's all about stuff coming out, so to speak. Every fast I research is intensely concerned with notions of purity and cleanliness, and the need to flush out these supposed pollutants, whether through laxative teas and chugging a gallon of salt water, a technique that basically consigns you to the toilet for the better part of an hour, or, in my case, the enemas.

"We live in a dirtier and dirtier world, and yet our lives are longer and longer. Go figure," says Sanders, pointing out the central paradox at the heart of the fasts. But five to ten pounds of toxins? That's the size of a robust newborn baby. It seems like an awful lot of poison in an ostensibly healthy person.

"It seems unlikely," says Sanders. "Things you take into your system are incorporated into your cells, there's no question about that. That's why red dye number five has been banned. How long they stay there is not as clear. Our cells are pretty selective about what they take up as far as we've been able to tell."

Whatever the reasons, by Day Four I do feel much better, just as predicted. I go to the movies where a woman two aisles over has what appears to be an entire Chinese dinner right there in the theater and I do not mind. Later that same evening, I sit across from my friend Rick in a restaurant as he enjoys a perfect meal of a fancy pressed sandwich and a low dish of butterscotch pudding, washed down with a flute of prosecco with pomegranate seeds being batted about in its helix of bubbles. I am conscious of his food, but I don't feel ravenous as I drink my peppermint tea. At no point does he morph into a huge pork chop on legs. I am not hungry, and my headaches and listlessness are largely gone.

But that's it. No golden shafts of light piercing the clouds, no strange hallucinatory visitations. It's still early days yet, I know, but this lack of something larger has me feeling a little concerned. Perhaps I'm doing it wrong. My fasting notebook recommends that I pass the fifteen minutes of holding my enema by reading some sort of spiritual literature. I have been opting for *The New York Times* instead. I cannot believe that staying engaged in the world is the thing standing between me and my glorious uptick. The accounts I've read and heard convince me that it is all but inevitable. Eventually there will be nothing for me to do but embrace this brilliant, beautiful thing that will overtake me, whether I like it or not. It has to happen. Physiology will out. I'm just not that special.

On Day Six I finally feel something unmistakably different, and it's not what I expected. I am up early, my energy is high. I feel great. I stand in the bathroom on top of the spread-out newspaper and give myself my weekly haircut. And then, suddenly, my heart begins to race. I am overcome with a shaky weakness and the distinct feeling that I cannot trust my body to do what it is meant to do. Or rather, that what my body is meant to do in that moment is to pass out and have me crack my head against the cold, unforgiving edge of the tub. My upstairs neighbor very kindly walks with me to see my doctor a block away. I buy a banana on the way, just in case everything goes to hell and I have to end this thing.

My blood pressure and my pulse are both normal. My doctor's not crazy about the idea of me fasting but tells me that I am essentially fine. I could, in fact, go for a good long time without food. I probably just had a moment of hypoglycemia. This reassures me and I go home. I drink a little extra juice and return to feeling fine in a matter of minutes. The banana sits on my table, an uneaten taunt, like Chekhov's loaded gun, introduced in the first act that must perforce be fired before the curtain comes down. I peel it, wrap it in foil, and stick it into the freezer out of sight.

I will not lie, there is a brief interval of joy while walking to the doctor, when I think I might be forced to return to the wonderful world of mastication, although I also know I would feel like a failure if I pulled out eight days early. Now that I am facing fully another week with my fast intact, I am back to square one, wondering how I will manage to get through this.

THE BROTH IS a beautiful ruby color and smells wonderful. I'm probably fooling myself, but it feels like I can taste the minerals, sense them rushing through my body, exerting their healthy, sustaining influence. I look forward to each mug as though it were a full meal. The broth has to be made every two days. It goes rancid if kept longer. It involves a good deal of washing, chopping, boiling, and straining. It clears my mind and allows me to think. It becomes a moving meditation. I'm turning everything into a moving meditation at this point. There's a slight desperation to this constantly taking the pulse of my world. I'm investigating and palpating everything, trying to find my way back to the bed in a dark, unfamiliar room. Is this my shiny, rosy-hued epiphany, my hands blindly searching in front of me? Is this?

Day Nine. Maybe this is it. I am curiously relaxed, as if my bones had been removed. It's wonderful, but it's a surface calm. I am still aware of my set of First World Problems and their underlying causes. It's not like I just now realize that they are trivial—I always knew they didn't amount to a hill of beans—but my physical anxiety response is gone. It is lovely, but hardly seems worth the effort. If this is all there is, then I hate to say it, but Miss Peggy Lee was kind of right. On the street, a bike messenger zooms by dangerously close to me, nearly shearing off my kneecaps. Where once I might have hissed it, I can now only mutter "Jerk." I cannot physically work myself up into a lather. Do I think, *Hello, fellow enbicycled human. Come, ride freely, let the wind carry you like a seedling, like a bird*? No, what I think is, *Schmuck. I hope you are crushed beneath the wheels of a bus.* But the difference is the venom that pulses through my veins now has the restful back-and-forth rush of the ocean's waves.

MY FASTING PROGRAM warns me to stay vigilant against unhealthy ego investment and unjustified feelings of superiority. Just because I am an ethereal creature of light and air I should take care not to pass by the falafel stand, for example, and look down disdainfully from my slender, Olympian perch at the weak-willed humans who feel the need to stuff their gullets with something as earthbound and disgusting as solid nourishment. I know what it's like to groove on avoiding food. I derive some of my deepest pleasure in life from forgoing pleasure. I get off on self-flagellation and various little acts of bourgeois penance, like doing my laundry or skipping meals. Especially skipping meals. But that's not about feeling superior to others so much as asserting a steely personal control. It's a white-hot fire of self-abnegating virtue which, when it overtakes me, is one of the great joys of my life. By all accounts, I should be having it now. I am not just taking in less food, I am taking in none. I am fully ten pounds lighter. But fasting hasn't lessened my usual feelings of venality and guilt.

If anything, it has increased them, what with my days being little more than a narcissistic rumination about my intake and, ahem, output. Between the hours of making the broth and giving myself the enemas, this is one of the most self-obsessed things I have ever done in my life, and I say that as someone who wrote an entire book about myself.

Apparently I also have to worry about the ego projections of others. Brian advises everyone to keep the fast to themselves. What I will find is that those who know I am fasting will broadcast their own worries or anti-fasting prejudices, saying things like "You look too thin," while those who don't will try unsuccessfully to put their finger on just why I look so uniquely healthy and great, like the Viagra commercial where people are struck by the charismatic confidence with which the newly bonerific fellow moves through the world. It seems true. My friends who know I am fasting think I look terribly gaunt, and not in a good way. One Saturday morning, I go to synagogue for the baby-naming service for the twins of some friends who have no idea. I've lost twelve pounds. I wait for the compliments. I find out later that someone asked my friend Jeff if I had cancer.

One night on the subway, I see a woman at the end of the car. She leans over to the people sitting near her and asks in a quiet, friendly, almost businesslike manner, "Do you have any extra food that I could buy off of you?" I can only hear her because the train is silent. From a distance, she doesn't look appreciably different from the rest of us. I wouldn't have picked her out. On closer inspection, I can see that her clothes are worn, and that what appeared to be a ruddy complexion is actually a dirty face. She isn't standing in the middle of the car addressing us. She is just asking those within earshot. I walk over and give her a dollar before I get off at Union Square. "But do you have any extra food?" she asks me. I don't, but I also know in that moment that there is neither clarity nor serenity enough in the world that would give me the chutzpah to explain to her why not.

DAY THIRTEEN, THE home stretch. I have lost fourteen pounds. I am not really hungry but I am experiencing appetite. I find myself thinking about food a lot; about cooking it more than eating it. I pore through books and surf the Web for recipes: roast goose with prunes, brown butter madeleines, candied grapefruit peel. Precisely the kind of Olde Worlde delicacies Hans Christian Andersen's Little Match Girl saw dancing before her eyes before she froze to death on the Copenhagen street.

On my final day without food, I bound out of my house, another blue and freezing day. The light of the city is etched with a diamond-bit drill. I am feeling jaunty and alive, like a character in a movie who, newly in love, walks through the streets he thought he knew, only to find them vibrant and full of beautiful humanity, and he a wonderful part of it all: he dances for a group of French children, he smiles with friendly commiseration at young couples, flirts nonthreateningly with an old lady, telling her, "Madam, you smell delicious!" But it is not universal brotherhood that has me jazzed as I dance along.

What I am thinking to myself is, *Hello world! Tomorrow I eat an apple!*

My high spirits are tempered with something else, though. When I tell Brian that I feel good but not markedly different, he doesn't hesitate to tell me that my experience is atypical. Part of the reason for this, he tells me, is the length of my fast. Apparently true detoxification and its attendant bonanza comes when one fasts the number of days of one's age plus seventeen. In my case, that would be close to two months of fasting. The twenty-day fast is the shortest one offered, it is true, but it *is* offered. In his later correspondence to me, Brian qualifies my fast more than once as "the very shortest," one that people can do "standing on their heads," and says that I just "dipped my toe in."

It strikes me as a little unsporting and kind of assoholic for him to paint my program as the fasting equivalent of Rosie Ruiz taking the subway during the Boston marathon. Mine, it seems, is the fast of the faker and dilettante. Apparently I might as well have been sitting around with a bucket of chicken and a TV remote. But it's more than just the piddling duration of my experience. Brian thinks I didn't approach this with an open mind from the beginning. He feels I had written the story in my head before I even started, looking to debunk him and the entire thing as pseudoscience.

In truth, we didn't get along from the start. In our initial phone call, when it came out that I was from New York, he said sagely, "Ah, the second most toxic city in the U.S."

"What's the first?" I asked.

"Los Angeles."

LA sounds reasonable to me, but New York City has no industry and is vertical and has exponentially fewer cars than anywhere else. Surely some of those rust belt towns are dirtier, I wonder aloud. Brian is not pleased with my doubting him and responds shortly, "Steel is done as an industry and you have ten million people."

I let it rest, but I can't help thinking, *10 million people with mass transit.* I think he's wrong and I do a little research. According to the EPA, just in terms of air quality, New York ranks fourteenth, not second. I feel Brian is speaking about some other kind of chimerical toxicity; the New York stereotype of the city as a cynical, New Age–free zone.

After that, our e-mail exchanges seem to follow a similar dynamic. He finds me annoyingly inquisitive and his impatience makes me feel like I've been insubordinate. He is curt and resorts to a lot of uppercase spelling, which I think is meant to seem exuberant and expansive but in e-mail just means yelling. In fact, all of his e-mails seem rife with barely concealed anger at me. He reminds me of the menacing gym teachers of my youth, while I no doubt remind him of some pedantic pansy ruining everybody's fun with my constant interrogation and fear of the ball.

But I am determined not to let our bad relationship be the story. I try to keep our communication to a minimum and whatever contact we do have, I keep as chatty and neutral as possible, resorting to the age-old tactic of talking about the weather. Good thinking on my part. It gets back to me later that Brian tells other people that "David wimped and whined his way through his fast, complaining constantly about his freezing New York."

It's a fairly bleak and isolating feeling when your own guru hates you.

RETURNING TO THE world of digestion must be done gradually. Before the apple I am to have some broth mixed with a tablespoon of bran and flaxseed, to give it some bulk and prepare my body for anything with mass. It is like thin porridge. I crunch down on the seeds, the first chewing I've done in fourteen days. It takes me almost twenty minutes to swallow eight ounces of liquid, and it leaves me depleted. I have to go back to bed for an hour and a half.

My apple, to which I had so looked forward, now just seems like an immense ordeal. I had bought myself the hardest, sourest Granny Smith for the occasion. I had imagined a gusto-filled chomp, the sound of my teeth breaching its skin and flesh gorgeous music to my ears, but now the thought is only exhausting. I cut the fruit up into careful, grandmotherly slices. I bite into the first one tentatively. The more I chew the easier it becomes. A third of my way into it, I am tearing into my first meal as if I had never even been away from eating at all. The flavor is sublime, but there's an undertaste of bitterness, too. I hardly need Brian's dislike of me to feel like I blew it, as though I returned from a trip to Paris only to find that I had somehow missed everything, and hadn't even noticed they spoke French there. I cannot shake this sheepish feeling that

I somehow failed to receive the thing I should have, and here I am, already out the door and it's too late.

When I started the fast, I had entertained the romantic notion that it wouldn't just work but that it really would be the magic bullet. The fast would short-circuit logic and somehow my problems, such as they are, didn't need the talk and the scrutiny, they needed this. There was even a moment where I thought I could see all those self-generated impediments, feel them even, impacted and concentrated into a gray, plaquelike obstruction: a thick, squat blockage the shape and size of a scallop, plugging up some critical channel of my body. I thought, I hoped, that *this* was the way they might finally be broken up, pulverized, and flushed away.

It can be hard to remember what one's anticipatory image of something was once you're on the other side. I'm no longer sure exactly what it was I was waiting for, but I do know that it was something wholly unfamiliar and thrilling. Like a new color. Not a mixture, no trace of blue or yellow or red. What would that look like? I have some basic understanding about light—how it can only be broken down and refracted into its seven constituent hues—and even though I know that the physical world makes the existence of such a thing basically impossible, I'd still really like to see that.

OFF WE'RE GONNA SHUFFLE

The Grim Reaper cannot catch a break in Newport Beach, California. In a grand ballroom of the Marriott, a slide of the hooded, scythe-wielding one shows him imprisoned behind a circle with a diagonal strike through it; international sign of negation. Adding insult to injury, he has been rendered with juvenile simplicity. The Pale Rider looks like a neutered Milquetoast. He could signify "No trick-or-treaters!" for all the menace he musters. This vanquished monster is the visual for a lecture entitled "Death Is an Outrage!" being given by a man named Rob Freitas.

"During the time I just spoke this sentence, a dozen people died," he says, sounding duly appalled. He pauses for effect, and then adds, "And there's another dozen," throwing his hands out like an exasperated parent with an impatient *Happy now?* gesture. The scratch of pens on paper fills the room as people transcribe Freitas's words. It's an Escher-like moment, the cereal box with an image of a child eating cereal beside a box with an image of a child eating cereal beside a box, and so on. *How many people died,* one wonders, *in the time it took to write down what he said about how many people died in the time it took him to say it?*

The Extreme Life Extension Conference is a three-day meeting sponsored by Alcor, the Scottsdale, Arizona, cryonics company that has Boston Red Sox Hall of Famer Ted Williams in cold storage, with hopes that he may one day rise again. Like worshippers at a weekend-long Easter Mass, about 150 scientists and acolytes have gathered to hear the Good News about the latest developments in securing their own resurrection and immortality. Death hovers over everything here, although less as an awe-inspiring, numinous presence than a nuisance, a persistent midge to be batted away. Death is not going to ruin anyone's picnic. As chair Ralph Merkle, a nano-technologist from Palo Alto, puts it simply, "This conference is about, by, and for people who think life is a pretty good thing and that more life is better." Even the landscape surrounding the hotel seems optimistic: rolling manicured lawns, palm trees, and flower beds planted with murderously orange canna lilies, sloping gently down to the emerald golf links of Orange County.

Rob Freitas continues. "This holocaust we call natural

death produces 2.4 million deaths annually in the United States alone. The human death toll in 2001 was nearly 55 million people. The worst disasters in human history *pale* in comparison to natural death. The flu epidemic of 1918 was less than half the toll from natural death." Freitas goes on to liken the richness of each person—his knowledge and experience, as opposed to, say, the street value of his hair and gold fillings—to the equivalent of at least one book. That's a "destruction" equivalent to three Libraries of Congress per year. Further, if you agree that some people are more than one book, then it's even more devastating. If, however, you feel that some folks' book is *The Prince of Tides,* or that others of us add up to all the complexity of a document, frequently pink, entitled "While You Were Out," then it's a tragedy of lesser magnitude.

Like Ralph Merkle and many here, Freitas is a nanotechnologist. Nanotechnology is the Holy Grail of what's to come for cryonics. It will be nanotechnology that will make bringing people out of cryosuspension possible. He paints a picture of a future in which an array of intelligent nanodevices will be dispatched into our bodies like so many *Fantastic Voyage* Raquel Welches, their sole mission our intracorporeal perfection. Many of the methods are already theoretically feasible: chromosome replacement therapy (microscopic cell-by-cell damage repair), respirocytes (artificial red blood cells that would enable us to sink to the bottom of a pool and hold our breath for four hours), microbivores (artificial white blood cells that would be one hundred times more effective than the real thing). All of these, says Freitas, could potentially restore us to the perfection of youth.

"A roll back to the physiology of your late teens might be easier than your ten-year-old self," he says, "and more fun. We could live about nine hundred years."

A libidinous thrill ripples through the crowd as they pick up on Freitas's erotic innuendo. It's almost poignant, this desire to return to the ruthless food chain of those miserable years. The grand fantasy of cheating death has wiped their memories of high school clean, because one need only look around the room to know that many of the attendees must have spent a good portion of their late teens being forcibly hung from coat hooks by their underpants.

MOST EVERY CULTURE has a cautionary tale about some soul who forgets his place and aspires to godlike powers only to be brought low as a result. The muddle of Babel and the disastrous hubris of Icarus are not invoked here, no surprise. What is brought up as a worthy precedent for cryonics is a 1773 letter from Benjamin Franklin: "I should prefer to any ordinary death, being immersed in a cask of Madeira wine, with a few friends, till that time, to be then recalled to life by the solar warmth of my dear country."

Aside from its implausibility, Franklin's dream of pickling shares a crucial passivity with the modern cryonics movement, both being dependent on the ministrations of others to bring one back. As for proactive, personal efforts at extending the life they have now, I don't see a whole lot of it beyond a woman with a ziplock bag full of herbal supplements. I never see, for example, anyone else in the hotel gym. Over the three days of the conference, I am the only one in the fitness center doing this particular tap dance along the mortal coil. Instead of breathless conversation, my soundtrack is the whir of my solitary treadmill and the neocon drone of Fox News on the television placed too high up for me to change the channel. I have heard the future and it sounds like Bill O'Reilly.

There is a lecture about the fifty ways in which we might potentially slow our aging, including switching from coffee to tea, doing weight training, and cutting out fat and sugar, but people still seem perfectly happy to tuck into lunches of mashed potatoes, beef in gravy, chicken in cream sauce, and white-flour rolls. We eagerly line up for our life-extending Mexican buffet. I am reminded of that moment in *Sleeper*, when one of the scientists of 2173 is amazed to hear that Woody Allen, a health-food store owner revived out of cryosuspension after two hundred years, knows nothing of the salubrious properties of hot fudge. I have tasted the future and it is gooey with melted Jack cheese.

EVEN IF REANIMATION works—and conventional science likens such a prospect to reconstituting a live cow from a package of hamburger—progress is a continuum: there will inevitably be a good many botched thawings before they get it right. The brains of the first few subjects will likely have all the cognitive capacities of pimento loaf, with minds so amnesiac and compromised, reborn into a world whose technology so far outstrips our capacity to ever come up to speed, that the only life available would be as a menial. And I also cannot get past thoughts of the crushing loneliness of waking up years hence without loved ones, knowing nobody. Gregory Benford, a physicist and science-fiction writer, suggests having one's "context"—friends and family—frozen alongside one. One would then be reanimated into a community of like-minded cryonauts. But even without them, Benford argues, the future will be no worse than a new infancy. "When we're born we don't know anybody. Others know us, though. It's like being a star."

To render this eventual stardom a less threatening prospect—to make us feel it as something closer to the glow of adoration we might encounter at a movie premiere, say, rather than the notoriety that will lead torch-wielding villagers to storm the castle calling for our monster heads—we are given a pep talk by a man named Max More. More is a leading proponent of transhumanism, a philosophy dedicated to the superpositive but rather diffuse goals of extending life, advancing without limits, and achieving heretofore unimagined heights of human potential, all through technology. Like many utopians, he has adopted a pseudonym, in his case one meant to embody all the hypertrophic dynamism of this brave new world; 150 years ago, he would have been calling himself Hieronymus T. Steam Engine. More and his wife, Natasha Vita-More (get it?), are the golden couple, the Scott and Zelda of the conference, he with his ponytail, muscled physique, and equine haunches packed into tight jeans, she as sleek as a hood ornament in a white pantsuit.

He calls his process of mental preparation for the future

"deabyssification," but aside from the rather catchy buzzword, it is content-free miasma. Essentially, he tells us to expect the unexpected. To simulate the unknowability of what's to come, he suggests we "use psychological tools. Keep throwing yourself curves. Start your own business. It's about being healthy, vibrant, and alive, and challenging yourself." Even in this audience of believers, people are detecting the distinct slipperiness of snake oil on their tongues. Their abyss is in no way diminished. Eventually someone tries to pin More down and asks him about his own specific thoughts of what the future will be like. More demurs, saying that were he to tell, his version would unhealthily influence others' vision and we'd all be stuck using the same derivative tropes (more derivative and tropey than "push yourself out of your comfort zone," I'm guessing).

If this is what passes for prescriptive information, it's really no wonder that these brilliant scientists seem so clueless. They may be up on their molecular engineering, tissue preservation, and protocols in the rapid cooling of bodies, but ask them something mundane, like where reanimated Alcorians will get their money, and the blank stares begin. At other times, the flights of fancy are straight out of a bedtime story. During a lull between speakers, a sixtyish elfin man named Peter Toma stands up at the microphone. Toma, a finely made European linguist and pioneer in the field of automatic translation programs, tells of being disconsolate when his mother was dying, believing "there must be a continuation of life." He tried to find some place to store her body, looking in New

Zealand and Argentina, to no avail. She is now safely at Alcor. And today Toma bears great tidings. He has found a place where one can go into "vistasis"—that is, be frozen while still alive, although the process itself would kill you (Alcor's official position on vistasis is one of supportive non-endorsement). This magical place? Switzerland. I am shocked, *shocked,* to hear that the Swiss—whose famous neutrality has made them a shining beacon unto the world for haven-seekers, clock enthusiasts, and Nazi bankers—will, according to Toma, look the other way if one is euthanized within their borders. Switzerland has other advantages should some unforeseen global disaster arise. "We can be taken into the mountains." I can hear the strains of Grieg and the plinking of icicle chandeliers, as bobsledding teams of dedicated scientists, their frozen cargo carefully loaded onto sleighs, mush their way through the ever thinner air, up, up into craggy hideaways. "So!" Toma concludes his alpine fairy tale. "Switzerland!"

THE AREA AROUND Alcor headquarters in Scottsdale is dominated by low buildings in ochre-colored plaster. It's hard to distinguish the Chinese buffets from the stone-and-marble suppliers from the cryonics labs out here in this vast Frederic Remington landscape. Alcor itself is a one-story box of a place, set back from the road by a small parking area and a gravel desert garden, with palmettos and agave plants. Almost defiantly unprepossessing, it could be a suburban dental practice. There would be no way of knowing that this is the temporary resting place for the dead in Scottsdale. Then again, there is also no way of knowing until you visit that the terms "temporary resting place for the dead" and "Scottsdale" turn out to be cruelly synonymous.

On a round glass table in the modest reception area sits an Emmy Award, part of the bequest of Dick Jones, a writer for *The Carol Burnett Show*. The familiar sharp-winged angel, already a quarter of a century old, is showing a tracery of crackle on her electroplate finish. A statuette is not a sculpture; it *belongs* to someone. It looks misplaced, as if the owner might come back at any moment. Jones is also among the twenty-odd Alcor patients who have opted to have their pictures displayed in the entrance. He was a handsome man and the small brass plate underneath his photo bears his name, as well as the dates of his "first life cycle." Other photographs include a man holding the hands of his wife who, it seems, is still alive. An older couple in their forties Sunday best. A young man, dead at age twenty-nine from hemophilia-derived AIDS. There is very little fanfare to this gallery. They could all be Employees of the Month.

It's neither terribly difficult nor terribly expensive to sign up for cryonic suspension. There is a lot of paperwork, much of it in triplicate and much needing to be notarized. Bodies are bequeathed to Alcor under the Uniform Anatomical Gift Act, the same statute that allows you to give your postmortem organs to the sick, or donate your cadaver so that first-year anatomy students can cut you up and, if my cousin's medical school experience is any indication, make fun of the size of your penis. Suspensions are paid for by insurance policies taken out with Alcor as the beneficiary. It costs $75,000 for a neuropreservation, "neuro" for short, which is just your head, and $130,000 for your whole body. Ted Williams, our most famous frozen American, is a neuro. (That apocryphal tale of Mr. Disney being preserved in a secret laboratory somewhere underneath Main Street, USA, is a myth, I'm afraid. Uncle Walt was summarily cremated upon his death in 1966.)

Membership also comes with a one-foot-cubic box for memorabilia and keepsakes, which is placed one mile underground in a salt mine in Hutchinson, Kansas. Patients receive a Medic Alert–type bracelet, as well as a dog tag on a neck chain and a wallet-sized card, all with the express written admonition that no autopsy be performed in the event of your death. If any cutting is going to be done, that's Alcor's job. And if you're a neuro, there is some major cutting to be done, namely decapitation, euphemistically referred to as "cephalic isolation."

Alcor's primary competitor is the Cryonics Institute in Michigan. Suspension at CI costs considerably less at $28,000, and they emphatically do not offer a head-only package. As they say on their website, "Few things have served to caricature and discredit cryonics so thoroughly as neurosuspension." Alcor, in turn, feels that CI is not as scientifically advanced. CI rebuts that Alcor's insistence on niceties such as surgical sterility are merely cosmetic, conferring a "medical look" while driving up costs.

This rivalry is squabbling over an anticipatory dream, like the old joke about the family that gets into pitched battle about the car that hasn't been bought yet. "This is the realm of science fiction," says a scientist at the National Nanotechnology Initiative at the National Science Foundation, who will not even allow himself to be named for a refutation. The extraordinary advancement that will have to have taken place before reanimation is remotely possible is multi-partite: there has to be a cure for the disease that killed you (or anyone else in suspension, meaning essentially a cure for every known malady); aging itself has to be arrested and reversed; the cellular damage from the extremely toxic cryoprotectant chemicals has to be reparable, as do the inevitable shatter injuries from the freezing itself; and in the case of neuros, there is the small added matter of somehow growing a new body to house your brain, possibly through therapeutic human cloning (stem cells). For now, cryonics remains a science of antecedence, as if anesthesia had been discovered centuries before the advent of surgery and scores of patients were just lying about on gurneys, out cold.

I am walked through the place by Hugh Hixon, the facilities engineer. Hixon is the longest-standing Alcor employee, having started there in 1982. He has participated in close to fifty suspensions. White-haired, bespectacled, and dressed in snug khaki shirt and trousers, he looks like a docent in the reptile house. He speaks somewhat slowly, with a flattened affect. When I ask him if it feels strange to work day in and day out in such close proximity to dead bodies and severed heads, he replies that it doesn't bother him much. His concentration is on the smooth technical operation of it all. "It helps that I'm a notably unemotional person," he concedes. "If I had a family, that might not be an advantage." Hixon's sangfroid is no posture, because he does have a family. Here on the premises, in fact. One of the photographs on the wall is his own father.

Hixon leads me through the cryonic process. Once your body has been safely transported to Alcor, it is saturated with antifreeze-like cryoprotectants and you are cooled to −230°F. In preparation for your long-term suspension, your temperature is gradually brought farther down to that of liquid nitrogen, −320°F (done too quickly and you'd shatter like an NBA backboard). Finally, you are moved into one of Alcor's dewars, the reinforced stainless steel tanks named after Sir James Dewar of the scotch-producing dynasty. There, you will wait out the years until the glorious flowering of science brings you back.

The five dewars, enough to hold the roughly sixty patients currently in suspension, are kept back in the patient care bay, a garagelike room. At capacity, a dewar can hold up to four full bodies and five heads. There are also a few suspended beloved cats and dogs scattered here and there throughout the dewars, wherever there's a bit of room. In the interests of space, pets are always neuros. Standing near these tanks, I have a hard time remembering that there are human bodies, and parts thereof, in them. There is no sinister hiss of liquid nitrogen. It's not even particularly cold, with none of that ozone smell of frigidity like in a hockey arena. If there is an overriding aroma to the place, it is coming from the small employee kitchen. I have smelled the future and it is redolent of microwave popcorn.

I ask Hixon whether any concessions are made to preserve

the neuros' faces. Not really. Neuropreservation is about the brain pretty exclusively. It is not extracted from the skull only to minimize damage to the structure. The hair is removed to reduce any insulating properties it might have and to allow easier access for the burr holes made in the skull for the crack-phones—seismograph-like sensors that monitor any fissures that might result from the freezing. Also, the antifreeze renders the skin translucent. "This is not a cosmetic procedure," is all Hixon will say on record.

My ghoulish line of questioning is less an attempt to get a rise out of him than to get one out of myself. It doesn't work. The whole place seems quite banal, which isn't that surprising. Every business, no matter how out there, gets its filing cabinets, faux-woodgrain desks, and half-wall partitions from the same few suppliers. It's not like I had been expecting the dark, heavy draperies of an Alistair Crowley decadence—ravens and human-skull wall sconces—but maybe a little chilly steeliness of *Gattaca* might have been nice. Something that would indicate what was actually going on here.

Efforts are being made to convey precisely that. At the time of my visit, a Hollywood set designer was already in the process of redecorating. The barnlike door that leads to the cool-down room will look like a large industrial freezer. The walls will be a two-tone affair of wainscot-high aubergine, topped by an elegant gray, and the dewars themselves might be moved into a more photogenic bowling-pin formation. They will also sport a gleaming mirror-bright surface. Hixon couldn't care less about these cosmetic changes, but he takes them in stride. "People seem to get turned on by the polished finish."

As I make my way to the stark white operating theater, I stumble upon a room with a large machine that bears a two-foot-long shaft, ending in a saw-toothed wheel about five inches in diameter. The teeth point both up and down in a fairly ragged and aggressive display of tear-apart force. Is this the decapitator, I wonder? No. It's a huge mixer, a kind of gargantuan Hamilton Beach they use to blend the very viscous cryoprotectant. When I ask Hixon to show me the cephalic isolator, he smiles and sighs gently, used to people's fixation on the "yuck factor." He takes me into a room walled in supply cabinets, opens one, and takes out a very ordinary hand saw, wrapped up in absorbent blue surgical paper, labeled with a handwritten slip of paper "amputation saw." So it all comes down to this. The back-and-forth motion of a good old industrial-age blade, powered by that most primitive of devices: the human arm.

"But a scalpel's just as good," he tells me.

JERRY LEMLER, WHO is president and CEO of Alcor when I visit in January 2003, is in his fifties, bearded, balding, with traces of a Freud-like demeanor, possibly a remnant of his career as a psychiatrist, which he was until quite recently in Knoxville. His wife, daughter, and son-in-law also work at Alcor. They will all be neuros.

Lemler is a patient and friendly man, and the first person to posit a fully rounded vision of a cryonic future. He believes in the coming of "the Singularity." Coined by the mathematician Vernor Vinge, the Singularity is that point in the future when machines of greater-than-human intelligence will be created, outstripping by far the intellectual capabilities of man. These machines, in turn, will design and create even more intelligent machines, resulting in an unfathomable explosion of intelligence and advancement. Once consigned to the far distant future, the Singularity is now thought to be closer than previously imagined. Vinge himself puts it at no later than 2030.

And what does this mean for the cryonauts? According to Lemler, "Once we tap into the physiologic basis of memory, I think most will opt to be uploaded onto computer disks, which can have multiple copies sent out to various places in the universe, so that if one is destroyed by a cosmic pinball explosion somewhere, another instantaneously can come up and would have all the memories of that first person."

Our physical presence would be no longer. The body would cease to exist, which would alleviate the need to learn how to grow new ones for the neuros. We would exist in a state of perpetual virtual reality.

I tell him a future as a CD-ROM seems unutterably bleak. Lemler tells me my attachment to the body is a sentimental one.

"They're just transitory and rather poorly formed for safety's sake. Vehicles for our mind, which is the essence of the person," he says.

But what about new experiences?

A function of programs uploaded for our delectation.

How are children born?

"They're not. It's the end of population as we know it today. There won't be any need to do menial work," he says with the ebullience of the better-living-through-insert-techno-pipe-dream-here romantic.

Maybe not here in Scottsdale. But Lemler is speaking of something supposedly only twenty-five years hence. There are still vast regions of the globe whose technology even now barely extends as far as potable water. What about the majority of people in the undeveloped world for whom life remains nasty, brutish, and short? How is all this supposed to reach them? It is not. By design. I remind Lemler that at the conference, the Singularity was also referred to as a "technorapture." He understands what I'm getting at. A rapture by definition is a division of souls where some are called and some are left behind to perish in the Lake of Fire. "We're going to have that whether Alcor is here or not, whether cryonics is here or not. A good portion of the population is going to die off, there's no question about that, much as mankind has done for however many millions of years."

At least there is a welcome touch of regret in his voice. Ralph Merkle had opened the proceedings with the statement that "more life is better." It seemed like an unimpeachable axiom, until it became clear that he was referring fairly exclusively to those in attendance. When the less fortunate did come up, it was briefly, during a discussion of how much some of the nanotech innovations might cost. A scientist seated behind me stood up to joke, "I think we'll see a lot of bootleg third world respirocytes."

Oh, those funny Africans with their broken-record insistence on access to lifesaving medications! Lemler, a liberal, is something of an anomaly within the cryonics community, which I have been told anecdotally is about seventy percent libertarian. It makes sense that they would subscribe to that Platonic ideal of uninterrogated politics. The collective perception in Newport Beach was that this was a convocation of mavericks, fringe radicals doing things their way with no outside help. That libertarian myth of the Lone Wolf gets a little shaky when one turns on a working faucet, stands under a lit streetlight, or realizes that every one of us got here by driving vehicles filled with highly subsidized foreign oil along a governmentally maintained freeway system. It is a troubling and downright inaccurate no-fault view of one's disproportionate allocation of privilege in this world. Why, it's consequence-free and limitless! More life is better!

And if it's simply a matter of cryonicists having a Rabelaisian vigor that compels them to seek years beyond their natural allotment, how does that jive with the Singularity scenario of a future as a computer disk, unable to experience anything new or organic? Why would one bother?

ROB FREITAS SAID in his lecture, "If you're physiologically old and don't want to be, then for you, aging is a disease." But that's not true, either philosophically or histologically. The equating of catastrophic illness with no longer being able to fuck like a jackrabbit goes to the very heart of the problem. It's that prototypical baby boomer trick of pathologizing those things that stand in the way of one and one's desires, however unrealistic or selfish.

Another of the lecturers ran through all the usual antilife extension bromides and arguments. One of them was that aging is good "because it gives life its meaning." This occasioned derisive snickering in the room. A joke I fail to get. Aging *does* give life some of its meaning, if you're lucky. Those changes in our bodies—the masteries that are acquired, the capacities that dissipate, the people we love and lose along the way—all form the basis of wisdom. They provide a sense of consequence and context. I feel fairly comfortable characterizing as sad, for example, that a man as old as Hugh Hefner still seems to aspire to nothing higher than dating twenty-four-year-old twins. Seven and a half decades is an awfully long time in which to not grow up. When is it enough? Why are we coming away from the table—laden with a plenty never seen before in human history—still feeling so hungry?

The Alcorians will think me a fool, no doubt, and there are many things in this world that are an outrage, to be sure, but death at our current life expectancy doesn't strike me as one of them (and as a gay man who lived in New York City during the eighties, I know a thing or two about people disappearing before their time). Maybe I sound like some Victorian who felt that forty years ought to be enough for any man, but one of the marks of a life well lived has to be reaching a state of finally getting it, of not needing more, and of being able to sign off with something approaching peace of mind. From that distance, shouldn't an empty tribute like an Emmy Award be just about the last thing you'd even think of putting on your table?

Given the choice, I'll throw my lot in with the rest of us whose deaths will be irrevocable, we Dustafarians. In my brief glimpse of what is to come I realize how little I care to witness it. I have seen the future and I'm fairly relieved to say, it looks nothing like me.

Acknowledgments

I am grateful to many people who helped to make happen much of the writing herein. All certainly helped to make it better. Alphabetically, they are: Kate Betts, Lindsay Borthwick, Alex Blumberg, Blue Chevigny, Diane Cook, Mary Duenwald, Andrew Essex, Ira Glass, Susan Lehman, Joel Lovell, Laura McNeil, Jim Nelson, Julie Snyder, Mim Udovitch, and Andy Ward.

At Doubleday, I was coddled by the wise Bill Thomas, indulged by the serene Kendra Harpster, cleaned up beautifully by Karla Eoff, and kept out of the hoosegow by Amelia Zalcman. Thanks also to Christine Pride, the twenty-something Rachel Pace, and, as always, the lovely Adrienne Carr-Sparks.